"This is the kind of book you wi   ach
new season of raising kids."

—Ma   ....onal

"Without question, *The Messy Life of Parenting* is one of the best parenting books ever. Seriously. I laughed. I cried. I fist-pumped on a regular basis while reading this fantastic book. Lori brings wisdom, wit, and wonder to every parenting scenario."

—Kurt W. Bubna, pastor and author

"Do you want to interact with your kids in a way that deepens your relationship, encourages responsibility, draws grace into the family fold, and molds a humble countenance? Then devour these pages now. Family connections matter to everyone now and into the future. They're worth the investment. Lori will show you how."

—Dr. Kathy Koch, founder and president of Celebrate Kids Inc. and the author of *8 Great Smarts* and *Screens and Teens*

"There is no underlying message of: 'If you had just tried harder, you would have amazing kids!' No. This book, with every shred of Lori's wisdom and grace wrapped up inside, gives you real-life, loving strategies to strengthen the family you have, no matter where you are starting from today."

—Kathi Lipp, bestselling author of *The Husband Project*, *Overwhelmed*, and *Clutter Free*

"Crud happens. Heartbreaks and hassles are an inevitable hazard of family life. Parents need a plan for seeing the big picture, and *The Messy Life of Parenting* delivers that plan."

—Jay Payleitner, national speaker and best-selling author of *52 Things Kids Need from a Dad* and *What If God Wrote Your Bucket List?*

"*The Messy Life of Parenting* is not only a powerful parenting book, but it's a grace-filled, common sense manual for life."

—Mary DeMuth, author of *Building the Christian Family You Never Had*

"*The Messy Life of Parenting* encourages, challenges, and equips parents to intentionally develop a family culture of loving interdependence in order to raise respectful, responsible children who receive and give the grace-filled truth that 'everybody spills.'"

—cohosts of the Grit 'n Grace podcast, Amy Carroll, Proverbs 31 Ministries speaker and author of *Breaking Up with Perfect*, and Cheri Gregory, author of *Overwhelmed*

"Lori Wildenberg offers practical ways to connect with your children, grow them in godliness, and steer them from isolated independence toward unified interdependence and lifelong relationships with one another. Treasure her help on your parenting journey, regardless of your children's ages."

—Cindi McMenamin, national speaker and award-winning author of *When Women Walk Alone, Drama Free, When a Mom Inspires Her Daughter,* and *10 Secrets to Becoming a Worry-Free Mom*

"*The Messy Life of Parenting* perfectly describes every parent's journey—*messy!* Life gets messy and days get long and hard. Thank you, Lori, for stepping out in faith to bring wisdom to all the mothers of the world. We needed to know we weren't in this thing alone!"

—Jennifer Maggio, chief executive officer, The Life of a Single Mom ministries

"Lori's book is full of encouragement to never lose hope, always pursue the hearts of your children, and no matter what—keep your eyes on Jesus!"

—Dr. Rob Rienow, Visionary Family Ministries

"Life is messy and complicated. The challenges facing our children are diverse and daunting. What we desperately need today is connection and commitment to relationships in the family. *The Messy Life of Parenting* brings this timely message to us."

—Ed Miller, director of development, National Center for Biblical Parenting

"Life is better when family relationships are close, and Lori is a trusted guide to walk with you on that journey."

—Josh Mulvihill, PhD, executive director of church and family ministry at Renewanation and founder of GospelShapedFamily.com

"We all have messes in our lives. *The Messy Life of Parenting* is written with you and me in mind. It is filled with practical insights but, more importantly, biblical wisdom that will allow God to turn our messes into miracles."

—Cavin Harper, founder and president, Christian Grandparenting Network

The MESSY Life of parenting

Powerful and Practical Ways to Strengthen Family Connections

by
LORI WILDENBERG

NEW HOPE
PUBLISHERS

BIRMINGHAM, ALABAMA
AN IMPRINT OF IRON STREAM MEDIA

Other New Hope books by Lori Wildenberg

Messy Journey: How Grace and Truth Offer

the Prodigal a Way Home

New Hope® Publishers
5184 Caldwell Mill Rd.
St. 204-221
Hoover, AL 35244
NewHopePublishers.com
An imprint of Iron Stream Media

Library of Congress Cataloging-in-Publication Data for *The Messy Life of Parenting* was previously filed as:

Names: Wildenberg, Lori, author.
Title: Messy parenting : powerful and practical ways to strengthen family connections / Lori Wildenberg.
Description: Birmingham, Alabama : New Hope Publishers, an imprint of Iron Stream Media, [2018] | Includes index.
Identifiers: LCCN 2018028518| ISBN 9781563090417 (permabind) | ISBN 9781563090547 (Ebook)
Subjects: LCSH: Parent and child—Religious aspects—Christianity. | Families—Religious aspects—Christianity. | Child rearing—Religious aspects—Christianity. | Parenting—Religious aspects—Christianity.
Classification: LCC BV4529 .W5543 2018 | DDC 248.8/45—dc23
LC record available at https://lccn.loc.gov/2018028518

All scripture quotations, unless otherwise indicated, are taken from the Holy Bible, New International Version®, NIV®. Copyright © 1973, 1978, 1984, 2011 by Biblica, Inc.™ Used by permission of Zondervan. All rights reserved worldwide. www.zondervan.com The "NIV" and "New International Version" are trademarks registered in the United States Patent and Trademark Office by Biblica, Inc.™

Scripture quotations marked (NASB) are taken from the New American Standard Bible®, Copyright © 1960, 1962, 1963, 1968, 1971, 1972, 1973, 1975, 1977, 1995 by The Lockman Foundation Used by permission.

ISBN-13: 978-1-56309-149-0

Printed in the United States.

1 2 3 4 5—22 21 20 19 18

This book is dedicated to

all parents who hope

for a relationship with their kids

that reaches beyond the

home and stretches into eternity.

Love endures forever,

Lori

Acknowledgments

With a heart filled with love and affection, I want to express my gratitude to my supportive, encouraging, and ever-growing family: my hubby Tom, my kids, Courtney, Jake, Samantha, and Kendra, along with my daughter-in-love Jaime and our sweet Sarah. I love it that we do life together.

To two encouraging and wise women who show me how it's done: my mom Pat Appel and mother-in-love Marianne Wildenberg Schmitt. I am grateful for your example.

To my steadfast friends, thank you for sharing your love and life with my family and me. You are there to cheer us on or ready to help us up: Julianne Adams, Shelley Appel, Maureen Behrens, Vicki Brock, Keri Buisman, Paula Calabrese, Becky Clark, Becky Danielson, Suanne Deskin, Jill Gillis, Paula Gleason, Gayle Hendrickson, Nina Hinds, Peggy Holland, Katie McElroy, Amy Raye, Darcy Robertson, Lindee Sebald, Stacey Van Horn, Kathy Wolfe, Elsa Wolff, Wendy Zueli, and Lucille Zimmerman.

To my Bible study buddies: Darcy Burdick, Diane Mueller, Barb Spencer, and Patti Vickers. Thanks for your support, prayers, and interest in this project. Each week I leave our time together refreshed and renewed. You are a blessing.

A big thank you to Ramona Richards and John Herring, with Tina Atchenson, Meredith Dunn, Reagan Jackson, and the rest of the New Hope family for recognizing the importance of interdependence and getting this message published. You are the best.

And to Jesus Christ, my Lord and Savior, the one who shows us how to have a relationship that lasts not just a lifetime but an eternity.

Contents

THE DECEPTION ABOUT CONNECTION

Be devoted to one another in love. —Romans 12:10

Life is filled with messes. We know it, yet we don't raise our kids like we believe it. Parents, we have been duped. And as a culture we have collectively savored and swallowed it. It is the lie regarding the virtue of independence. We have heard and even bought into the philosophy that our kids must learn to be, strive to be, independent. But what does that look like when life gets messy?

I can tell you that throughout my life I have had more than I can handle. You have too, haven't you? It is a certainty my kids and yours will also experience challenges and struggles along the way as well.

Eighteen straight months of more than I could manage replays in my mind. In January my dad died. In February I was in a ski accident and blew out my ACL. A few days later my middle daughter, Samantha, separated the bones in her foot while going over the hurdles in track. The two of us had surgery in March. And in June Murphy, the family labradoodle, was bitten by a rattlesnake. By August Samantha and I both needed a second surgery. In November Samantha, yes, the same kid, was in a snowboarding accident and experienced a concussion. In December our little Shih Tzu Bailey died, and in the same month, my son Jake and his college roommate were in a rollover car accident. The New Year started with Kendra, the youngest, rupturing her spleen in a near fatal snowboarding accident. Only hours after arriving home from the ICU, we visited Urgent Care when Samantha cut her hand and needed to be stitched up. By March Jake was diagnosed with an irregular heartbeat. Three of my four kids went to the hospital in an ambulance in a span of six weeks.

My nephew, Sam, told his mom he was going to quit telling his friends Wildenberg family stories because he was afraid they would think he was making it all up. And . . . I didn't even mention my oldest, Courtney, in this suffering synopsis because her story took a whole book (*Messy Journey: How Grace and Truth Offer the Prodigal a Way Home*).

Accidents, kids who wander, illness, and death all are a part of life. The life our kids will live will be similar; it won't always be happy and pain free. During those tough eighteen months, my husband Tom and I needed our family and friends. We depended on God. We would not have survived if we operated in an independent mode.

As Americans, independence surges through our veins. It speaks to our collective red, white, and blue blood. Old and young, liberals and conservatives, we all celebrate and believe in independence. We fight and die for it.

Naturally, the value of independence has seeped into family life. Parenting philosophies that support this idea are easy to spot. They teach strategies that focus on desirable behavior using logical and natural consequences: grab a rag and clean up the spill. They reward or punish acceptable or unacceptable behavior: if you don't spill you can have dessert but no dessert if you spill. The two basic premises are: if it's your problem, you fix it or do it right and get a reward; do it wrong and get a punishment. If a specific behavior, like potty-training or curfew abiding, is the only goal, these approaches work well.

But parenting is more than teaching obedience and appropriate behavior. A lot more.

While it isn't wrong or bad to parent this way, there is a better style, one that satisfies the longing for relationship in our parenting heart. Most of us moms and dads hope for more than simply good behavior. We want to grow our children's character while strengthening the family bond. In my opinion, a great and godly parenting strategy is relational. I want to interact with my kids in a way that deepens our relationship, encourages responsibility, draws grace into the family fold, and molds a humble countenance.

The natural consequence approach and rewards-punishment practice train the child to deal with life messes independent of their family. This misses the boat when it comes to building relationships, developing grace and mercy, and fostering empathy and compassion. Independence pushes relational intimacy aside. It ignores the support a family offers.

Is raising your child to be independent a paradigm you really want to practice? I think not. Most of us want a relationship with our kids that lasts a lifetime, one in which we are woven together throughout our lives and not just for the eighteen years of sharing the same living space.

I'm not talking about raising entitled, needy, and dependent kids. Sometimes we have trouble separating empowering from enabling. We want to raise our children to become responsible adults, to be people who can earn a living and support themselves. As a culture, perhaps we have commingled responsibility and independence, thereby getting an end result of independent children rather than simply responsible ones.

Life is to be experienced together—the good, the bad, and the ugly. I pray my children know they can come to their dad and me when they mess up, when they need a shoulder, an ear, or a hand (and a little less likely . . . some really great advice). Whether they are in the littles stage or the adulting phase, I want them to be confident in the knowledge that our family sticks together in the life spills because we are better together. Rather than raise a number of little islands, I prefer to grow a family more like a peninsula, where when grown, children are still connected by family interdependence based on a God dependence.

Two main lies fan the flames of the independent deception: "God helps those who help themselves" and "God doesn't give us more than we can handle." The other commonly held philosophy that adds fuel to the fire is, "I just want my kids to be happy." These two principles, plus the happy hope, are based on and give life to the independence lie and foster entitlement. None of these commonly uttered and sincerely believed statements are biblical.

The world can be a lonely place. God beckons us to call on Him and bids us to encourage and support one another. We are not meant to be solo souls. We are beings created for relationship with one another and with our Heavenly Father.

I want to live in a home where a family resides, one where people rely on one another, laugh with each other, share tears, and do life together. I want my kids to know, no matter what, they are part of a family that helps one another.

"It's your problem, you fix it," may promote personal responsibility, but it reinforces a go-it-alone mentality. Perhaps we don't use those exact crass words, but I bet most of us have said, "You spilled. You clean it up." or "You forgot your homework? Oh, so sad. I guess you'll have to figure out a way to solve your problem." (I am not talking about the habitual forgetter. That little rascal may need a dose of natural consequences.)

What if instead we responded to a life spill with, "That's OK. Everybody spills. I'll help you clean it up"? This phrase was heard at least three times a day in the Wildenberg household when our four kids were ages five and under. It wasn't a meal until somebody knocked over a glass of milk.

I'd like to appear noble and say the spillage statement came from thoughtful prayer and meditation. It didn't. It was strictly survival—mine. The spills were constant; no matter the preventive hoops I jumped through, the loosed liquid still splatted and spread. Those three lines helped me get through the potentially maddening moment.

This spillage parenting approach is our family philosophy. It communicates to our kids the three critical beliefs Tom and I hold: "That's OK—mom or dad won't freak out at life's spills. Everybody spills—normal life is filled with mess and mistakes. I'll help you clean it up." We want them to know no matter what, their dad and I are by their side.

Life is lived out in the unexpected—a statement that moves me to nurture the qualities of humility, empathy, responsibility, and compassion in my family. "That's OK. Everybody spills. I'll help you clean it up," sends the underlying message of grace and truth, "Our family is a grace-filled group of people who help each other out when life gets messy."

When kiddos are older, life spills make a bigger splash. It may look like a forgotten homework assignment or, like in my family, a car accident. "The car can be fixed. I'm glad you weren't hurt. Let's figure this out together."

It is music to a parent's ear to hear one sibling say to another, "That's OK, everybody spills. I'll help you clean it up." Independence frays family ties. An interdependent spirit knits our families closer as we deal with the unpredicted spills and wrecks together.

Throughout this book, we will discuss God's big idea for families and how we can strengthen and grow our kids by using a connected interdependent approach. We will examine God's design for loving others and loving Him. We will discover how to build up relationships in our families and how to encourage leadership skills in our kids. We will learn how to train our kids to be God chasers rather than people pleasers.

We will define the line in the sand between helping and enabling and identify the difference between empowerment and entitlement. We will learn to avoid the pitfall of poisonous praise and instead develop a mindset of challenge and perseverance. We will gain the tools necessary to discuss without division, correct without criticism, and maintain both convictions and relationship when in conflict.

And most importantly we will learn the secret of how to model God dependence to our kids.

I'm done falling for the independence lie. My goal isn't to raise independent children. My measure of success is to have responsible and caring kids who are able to rely on one another, ask for help and give help when needed, and trust the Lord throughout their lives. I don't want my young adults to become the Lone Ranger. I hope they will be more like the all for one and one for all Musketeers.

My intense eighteen months of constant challenge pales in comparison to the devastating experiences of other families. Just take the experience of one couple who gave their riveting testimony at my church. In just one year, they'd been through two bad vehicle accidents, a near drowning incident, a job loss, and a cancer diagnosis. Yet as they tell it, their story is more like Paul's in 2 Corinthians 11:16–33; they boast in their own weakness and God's strength. They glorify God for what He has done in the midst of their struggles and how fellow believers and family members support them.

Here's my boast. My dad is in Jesus' presence. Our little dog, Bailey, lived longer than expected. Samantha, Murphy (our labradoodle), and I healed. Miraculously, Jake was unscathed from the rollover and his roommate only sustained a broken finger. My son's heart rate returned to normal. Kendra not only survived her traumatic injury but has thrived and continues to snowboard. As my family walked through that time, God showed up big, family members stepped up for one another, and our friends were available with meals, kind words, and prayers. God used that season to illustrate the need for a committed family, strong friendships, and an unshakeable faith.

So it's no surprise I subscribe to the Spillage Parenting Philosophy—because it is OK when we spill. Spills happen to everyone, and it is very good when we help each other clean up the mess. Real life is not neat and tidy. The parenting adventure is a messy one.

Oh, and on a final note, all of the stories shared here and in the following chapters have each person's blessing and seal of approval.

On to the challenge of the messy life of parenting.

> *Finally, all of you, be like-minded, be sympathetic, love one another, be compassionate and humble.*
> *—1 Peter 3:8*

CHAPTER 1

THE ATTACHMENT TRUTH

Dear friends, since God so loved us, we also ought to love one another. —1 John 4:11

"Do you love me like I love my baby?" Maureen, a first time mom, was blown away by the love she had for her newborn. In an epiphany explosion, she realized her very own parents must love her the way she loves her infant. How can it be?

"I love you, babe." "I love you more," is my oldest child's go-to response. Courtney, my first baby, now a young adult, thinks she loves me more. I just laugh, "Yeah, sure."

The love of a parent for a child is beyond measure. The love equation is more of a love mystery. Moms, pregnant with their second baby, are often concerned they won't love the second as much as the first. One mom, ready to deliver any day, approached me after I spoke to her Moms of Preschoolers group. Her big brown eyes were brimming with tears.

"I'm afraid I won't love this baby like I love my first. I have been so busy with my toddler I've hardly even thought about this second one."

"The cool thing about love is that God always multiplies it; He never divides it," was my response. "God has already equipped you to love beyond what you imagine is even possible or logical."

Her fear is typical, but she can rest assured it will not be realized. She is doing old school human math, believing in the theorem that a finite amount of love is doled out at creation. Yet our loving God created love to mysteriously and supernaturally multiply and expand, never to divide and reduce.

We are able to give love because God first loved us (1 John 4:19). Our Creator shows us how. He gave us life, He gave us His Son. God first gives love and then we receive. That is how we know how to love. And that is why love has no limits. God and His love are limitless.

In the beginning, God created the heavens, the earth, and breathed life into dust, and the result was man, created in God's own image. Even though Adam fellowshipped with God, worked, and took care of Eden, Adam was not complete. "The LORD God said, 'It is not good for the man to be alone. I will make a helper suitable for him'" (Genesis 2:18). God waited a bit before He created Eve. First Adam had the task of naming the animals. Perhaps he had to realize his need for a more suitable companion before God created Eve. Adam, his humanity, his potential, his purpose, even his ability to reproduce could not be fully realized until Eve was made. God did not want Adam to be alone.

Being in relationship—loving God, and loving others—has been in our DNA since the beginning of time. We are created for connection. Helpers do life together and assist one another in spill reconnaissance.

Despite the fact that man was created for relationship, the great deceiver, dressed in snakeskin, crashed what God created as good and perfect. He led Adam and Eve to sin against God. Ever since then, work, relationships, childbirth, and the earth have suffered the consequences of Adam and Eve partaking in the forbidden fruit. The original perfect connection Adam and Eve had with each other and to God was forever tainted by the original sin (Genesis 3). Today we see that played out in our less than perfect relationships.

There are five types of connections family members may experience. Only one of the five fulfills Jesus' command to love one another. When Jesus speaks to His disciples, He also speaks to us. He said in John 13:34–35 that as He has loved us, so we must love one another. Christ's relational, sacrificial, and unconditional love is our example.

ZERO CONNECTION

The Lone Ranger sweeps in, saves the day, and rides off on Silver into the sunset. He completes his mission, exits the scene, and has no further connection with those he saved. Some families live like this: help when absolutely necessary and then remove oneself. The members live under the same roof yet live independent of the other individuals, and they only interact when absolutely necessary. The family is disconnected, and there is no long-term emotional investment. Compassion is replaced with callousness. The result of such an environment is withdrawal and resentment. Lived at its extreme, this is neglect.

Neglect is the most common type of abuse children suffer. Statistics show 62.8 percent of maltreatment cases are those who have experienced neglect. Neglect impacts relationships and attachment. It causes changes in the brain's wiring and can lead to attachment disorder, ADHD (attention deficit and hyperactivity disorder), PTSD (post-traumatic stress disorder), language delay, poor emotional development, and panic disorder. (These maladies are caused by other factors too. Just because a child has a diagnosis of ADHD does not mean he or she has been neglected.) Those results are from extreme cases. Although these disorders often manifest without neglect being present, the warning is there.

Human connection through nurturing is critical to brain development. Professor Allan Schore of UCLA emphasizes that brain cell development is a "consequence of an infant's interaction with the main caregiver (usually the mother)" and that brain growth "literally requires positive interaction between mother and infant. The development of cerebral circuits depends on it." The results of nurture are profound. Within the first two years of life, without the nurture of a primary caregiver, a child will not develop several aspects of brain function, including intelligence. We need to—we must—interact in order to grow and function.

Zero connection is something none of us want but many of us unintentionally encourage. We set up a lack of connection through distraction, inattention, and a chaotic schedule. Following church one Sunday, Tom and I went out for brunch. While we waited to be seated, I pulled out my iPhone and checked my email. Tom did the same. The other folks waiting were shoulder-to-shoulder with their companions,

CHAPTER 1

but no eyes met. Instead everyone was glued to the little screens on their handheld devices. Attention was diverted away from the real live person and given to scrolling and texting. Some were even on the phone talking to another person who wasn't even in their presence. I scanned the restaurant. Every booth, almost every table, had at least one if not more individuals distracted by their phone and not engaged with the people around them. Tom and I were as guilty as the rest.

Our devices can draw us away from being present. And we are getting closer and closer to ground zero of no connection and finding ourselves coasting on autopilot. We must be intentional about connecting face-to-face not just phone-to-phone. In order to flourish we need to be *with* each other when we are actually with one another.

One Sunday a month, Delaine's family gathers for dinner. Her family is made up of her husband, three adult daughters, their spouses, and the grandkids.

"When we started our once-a-month Sunday dinner tradition, I put a basket near the doorway. All iPhones, iPads, and electronic games are to be left in the basket as each person crosses the threshold. The devices safely reside in the basket until our evening concludes. At first my family grumbled a bit. But now if I forget the basket, they remind me."

Dinner at her house is a distraction- and phone-free zone. Delaine set up an expectation of how the evening would go, which is now appreciated and embraced by her family.

Disconnection or no connection occurs when we don't care, seek isolation, act like a victim, or rely on another person to maintain the relationship. As Delaine demonstrates, connection requires intention and investment.

TOXIC CONNECTION

Some may say something is better than nothing, but a toxic something is laced with poison. Think of Samson and his obsession with Delilah (Judges 16) or David and his fixation on Bathsheba (2 Samuel 11). Toxic connections function in the realm of extremes. And when that happens, somebody's going to get hurt. Sinful relationships always have a victim. Whether consenting or nonconsenting, intended or unintended, harm occurs in a toxic connection.

Carmen shares a story about her difficult relationship with her mom and dad.

"My relationship with my parents has been the most painful experience of my life. I was raised in a home where I was one of four kids. I was tucked right in between my siblings—an older sister, older brother, and a younger brother. We were very close.

"As a family we attended church every Sunday, but we did not talk about what it meant to be a follower of Jesus. Nice meals were on the table, consistent discipline provided, and material needs were met. I felt safe and loved. I am forever grateful for my early experiences.

"When my older brother was in high school he began to fight with my parents. As each of us grew and left home, it became increasingly difficult to get along with our parents. They made unkind remarks, criticized, and cracked jokes at our expense. If we brought our grievances to them they denied, justified, or passed them off as a joke. If we pressed the issue further we were disowned.

"After a while, the disowned adult child involved in the conflict would eventually show up at a family function. Everyone would pretend as though nothing had happened. The pattern continued for decades. A great deal of unresolved hurt piled up in our hearts.

"Years later, my beloved older brother died from heart complications. My parents made numerous hurtful remarks about the funeral and my brother. All the pain and frustration that simmered beneath the surface boiled up. It could no longer be contained.

"At a time when we needed each other the most, my family fell apart at the seams. My younger brother confronted my parents. They immediately disowned him. I followed suit and had the same result. I was so broken. I could not return to the unhealthy pattern of pretending nothing was wrong. I faced judgment and criticism from my sister because I was unable to let it go. My dad told me, 'You have failed me. I'm ashamed of you. You will suffer eternal punishment.' My mom refused to discuss anything at all.

"I was tormented by my decision and overwhelmed with guilt. I met with two different Christian couples, all older and wiser than me. I also sought a Christian counselor. I wanted so badly to follow Jesus yet I was unsure what that looked like in this situation. I desperately needed their wisdom, advice, and their prayers. Independently, all five of them spoke the same truths to my soul."

Carmen received a confirmation of healthy separation from the five wise souls she consulted. This was part of the remedy to move forward. Forgiveness was the main ingredient. She grieves the fact that reconciliation is not yet a part of her story. Sadly, her attempt to restore the relationship has met with resistance.

It is difficult to imagine parents pushing their child away. Toxic relationships, including parent-child relationships, drip with venom. The poison will make one sick if the antidote of forgiveness is not administered. Part of Carmen's healing has included a way to honor her estranged parents. She chooses to honor them through prayer and by living a godly life. While separated from her earthly parents, Carmen diligently seeks the Lord daily, "Even though my offer to reconcile was rejected, it opened the door for the Lord's love to fill the spaces in my heart. I'm not mad or sad as often. I put a stop to losing my life over my situation. My energy is invested in the good things the Lord has placed in front of me: my husband, kids, good friends, and my ministry. To the best of my ability I make sure my life and actions honor Him. Through this, I have come to know God better and recognize His voice more clearly. Although my earthly father rejects me, I am a beloved daughter of the King."

The pattern of Carmen's family of origin was control through verbal and emotional abuse and then abandonment. God can restore and renew all things when we are receptive. Her parents' hearts have hardened. They pridefully maintain their stand. Miraculously, God has broken the cycle in Carmen's nuclear family. Carmen's past and her wounding has not dictated her present or her future. She has been transformed to be the mom and wife God created her to be, breaking the generational chain of abuse.

It is easier for an outsider to identify physical abuse than it is to spot emotional or verbal abuse like Carmen has suffered. Most parents do not want to harm their children. Unintentionally, we do and say things that have the power to break our kids' hearts. Here are fifteen common ways we spit a little arsenic from our lips. These typically spouted words don't create the same interdependent effect "That's OK. Everybody spills. I'll help you clean it up" does.

Poison is spewed when we:

Discipline in anger: "You are grounded for life."
Criticize rather than correct: "That's a stupid way to solve that problem."
Lecture rather than discuss: "Blah, blah, blah . . ."
Express unreasonable expectations: "You are two, and you need to sit perfectly still during church."
Compare one sibling to another: "Your sister was able to [fill in the blank]."
Bring up past failures: "Remember when you [fill in the blank]."
Use sarcasm: Yeah, right, you are so smart."
Kill joy: "You could have done even better if you had [fill in the blank]."
Shame: "You are so clumsy."
Broadcast failures: "You won't believe what my son did."
Blame: "It's your fault I ran the red light."
Present ourselves as perfect: "When I was your age I never [fill in the blank]."
Steal success: "You got your talent from my side of the family."
Don't admit wrongdoing: "I'm the parent. I'm always right."
Never ask for forgiveness. (Ditto above.)

As we hold our child's heart in our hands, let's have a firm and gentle grip so he or she can thrive and become the person God created him or her to be. Even when we, as moms and dads, mess up or spill, it isn't too late—we can always adjust our approach, ask for forgiveness, and begin anew.

CONDITIONAL CONNECTION

Do you deserve my love? Have you earned my love? These are words a conditional connector says. I like to think I don't have conditions on my love. Yet as I examine myself I realize I have been guilty of verbalizing conditional love statements.

"You don't deserve a hug."

"You were so bad we are not going to [fill in the blank]."

"Because you misbehaved you will not get [fill in the blank]."

Conditional connections are all about performance rather than being. What a person does dictates acceptance, rather than who a person is.

Some families who appear very close are actually conditional connectors. These families are enmeshed and entangled. Emotional entwinement is not interdependency, it is codependency.

An enmeshed relationship is emotionally dependent. The members are constantly and highly involved in each other's lives. They feel threatened by another's personal growth, relationships, or independent choices. Emotional blackmail is used to keep the unhealthy relationship intact. Typically those involved in a codependent relationship have few outside friends. They discuss every decision and conversation with the other. Privacy is nonexistent. When one lives in an enmeshed family each individual feels as though he or she has to prove love for and loyalty to the family unit.

Sadly, if a family member of an enmeshed family unit challenges the status quo, often he is cut off and shunned by the rest of the members. Conformity is the name of the game. Control is the major player. The rules of the game are usually the parents' expectations.

To combat enmeshed parenting it is wise for moms and dads to also have their own interests and hobbies. It is easy to make idols of our children. But when we do, they have taken God's place in our hearts.

We desire to raise our kids to be successful, to own their values and ethics (even faith), and to develop their own personality and style. We want our kiddos to manage both their success and failure. As parents, we are not defined by either result. We hope our kids know our love and our relationship are not dictated by their performance. God lets us know He is not a conditional connector when He tells us He will never leave or forsake us (Deuteronomy 31:6). And that "While we were still sinners, Christ died for us" (Romans 5:8). (Thank You, God, for grace.) The message of grace is one our kids need to hear and believe.

When my son Jake was around eight years old, he asked me, "If I went to jail, would you stop loving me?" His question knocked me off balance.

"I'd love you no matter what." (A smarter mom would have followed up with a question or two.) Anyway, his inquiry was a heads up that I needed to deliberately communicate my unconditional love to my kids.

Conditional connectors remain in relationship only when everyone falls in line. Those relationships fall apart when belief and behavior collide. Parents who practice a conditional love approach might say, "Cut 'em loose," if what their child lives or believes is out of step with the parents' faith, morals, or values. Yet God says to never forsake. Differing beliefs can coexist. Our relationships don't have to be collateral damage.

SURFACE CONNECTION

Surface connections can be hard to spot, yet they reveal themselves when circumstances change. My dad and his brother, both now deceased, sadly had a surface connection. Once their parents died, the brother relationship dissipated. They had little to do with one another and only communicated as needed.

Typically one of the two in a surface relationship is more invested and is left hurt by the other's indifference. I have had relationships like this where I thought the bond was true friendship and then realized it was one-sided. That realization of a shallow connection can be heartbreaking.

Recently I observed a surface connection go under. This often occurs when the relationships are built on convenience, proximity, or perceived need. There were two friends, let's call them Christine and Hannah, with a group of four peripheral friends who were all in ministry together. You know, sort of friend-in-laws where the relationships come about by default. The group was Christine-centric. Once Hannah fell from Christine's favor and subsequently left the ministry, the others in the group dropped her too.

Hannah and I chatted about this painful dynamic. While we talked we recognized a pattern. This was not the first time Christine had ousted a person from the group. Hannah was most likely roadkill number five or six. Surface connections and relationships that are situationally based are devastating to those who thought they were deeper. We can spot people with the pattern of habitual surface relationships by noting how easily they discard and replace others. There is no movement toward restoration.

I don't want my kids to only connect because they share the same parents and grew up in the same home. As a mom it would break my heart, as I'm sure it did my grandparents, to have adult children who have no relationship with one another. Aside from parents, siblings are the only ones who share the same history.

A few years back I got some really bad counsel. It was advice I crumpled up and tossed right after I received it. During a very painful six-month time, my oldest Courtney was estranged from our family. She happened to be in a toxic relationship with a highly controlling partner.

Courtney withdrew from the family. One of the recommendations I received and rejected was, "Well, you raised her and now your job is done. You don't have to be in relationship with her anymore." This advice was not for me. I did the opposite. I continued to pursue my daughter so she knew beyond a shadow of a doubt she was loved, and her dad and I wanted her back in our lives. (By the way, Courtney did return to the family fold and ended that toxic relationship. Praise the Lord.)

"I don't know where I would be if my mom hadn't pursued me. Because she sought me out, I knew I could always come home." Courtney confirms that my continued pursuit was the thing that made returning home possible. (Thank You, Jesus.)

Judas had a surface connection to Jesus and the disciples. Even though Judas was a part of the twelve for three years, he was not truly connected or committed. When he realized his personal objective for power or wealth was not going to come to fruition, the surface connection showed itself in betrayal (Luke 22), a common result of this type of connection. Loyalty is only loyalty when there is commitment. Love, when it comes to counterfeit surface relationships, is not sincere.

INTERDEPENDENT CONNECTION

Dr. Barton Goldsmith in *Psychology Today* describes interdependent relationships as healthy and balanced. "The healthiest way we can interact with those close to us is by being truly interdependent. This is where two people, both strong individuals, are involved with each other, but without sacrificing themselves or compromising their values. What they have is a balanced relationship, and unfortunately it is not all that common. But it is attainable with just a little awareness and understanding."

Mostly I agree with Dr. Goldsmith with the exception that I believe love is sacrificial. I define sincere love as giving, loyal, and honest. Love blossoms where each party sacrifices for the other. Jesus said in John 13:34, "A new command I give you: Love one another. As I have loved you, so you must love one another."

God is love. Jesus embodies what that looks like. The Lord loves us no matter our response to Him. His heavenly love is pure, complete, and unconditional. Our fleshly bodies will never be able to fully and completely love unconditionally like Jesus.

The most satisfying human love isn't a one-way path; it is best when it is reciprocal, though not to the point where who did what is recorded on some sort of imaginary conditional love ledger. We give and receive because we want to—not out of obligation. An interdependent home is a place where the inhabitants can be real and transparent with one another because they know everybody spills. It's a safe place to fail and succeed, to discuss topics of substance and perhaps even disagree, to be accepted (even in the midst of disagreement), to be accountable to each other, and to be responsible for personal actions.

Just as Adam needed a suitable helper, we need helpers and companions in our lives. The psalmist refers to the Lord as a helper in Psalm 118:7: "The Lord is with me; he is my helper." Being a helper is an honorable and godly quality, not a lowly role. Think of what *helper* means: advocate, ally, comforter, companion, colaborer, coworker, participator, sustainer, and supporter. The word *savior* is even used as a synonym. There is honor in being a helper.

So yes, we really do get by with a little help from our friends—and from our family and from the Lord. Interdependency and a God dependency are threads I pray are knit into my family.

> *If either of them falls down, one can help the other up. But pity anyone who falls and has no one to help them up. Also, if two lie down together, they will keep warm. But how can one keep warm alone? Though one may be overpowered, two can defend them-selves. A cord of three strands is not quickly broken.*
> *—Ecclesiastes 4:10–12*

CHAPTER 2

HEALING THROUGH RELATIONAL TIES

Therefore encourage one another and build each other up, just as in fact you are doing. —1 Thessalonians 5:11

Bear Trap Ranch is a slow, seven-mile drive from Colorado Springs. The thirty-five minute, steep uphill dirt road ride (minus guardrails) requires navigating holes, rocks, blind curves, and carsick passengers.

This rustic, remote, and wooded ranch was the location for the Healing for the Soul Coaching and Pastoral Counseling weekend coaching retreat, which I attended as a staff member in training. I had the opportunity to learn from the best and watch God do His healing work with the clients who came. Most of the attendees had deep hurts from toxic messages given to them over the years. The time in the crisp mountain air was filled with pressing into pain in order to exhale hurt and move forward in freedom.

The drive to the location was the perfect mirror for the journeys these men and women had been on. They carried in their hearts and minds the cruel words spoken by those closest to them. It takes hard work and courage to uncover these types of wounds. Words may not break a bone, but they can critically injure a spirit. Words matter, and the closer the relationship the bigger their impact.

ACKNOWLEDGE THE WOUND

Even though time puts distance between the person and the pain, if a wound is not acknowledged it is difficult to heal and tough to move past. David Murray, in his article "Time Doesn't Heal All Wounds" for 1corinthians13parenting.com, admits his good intentions caused some hurt and resentment in his son. Many of us can regretfully relate to his story.

"I made the mistake of pushing too hard. . . . It is true that this led to great victories and life lessons, which have helped [my son] as a man, [but] there is now an emotional gap between us.

"I always said I never wanted to be like my father. He abandoned me as a child. He passed away (without an apology for the past hurt) and I must rely on God's grace to forgive . . .

"Now I look at my relationship with my oldest son and see a similar resentment. But unlike my father, my mouth still works. Recently it occurred to me that I have never said, 'I'm sorry.' *Why should I have?* I never felt guilty of any offense (which is always the problem).

"The two simple words, 'I'm sorry,' have unbelievable power. My wife is happy. [My son] knows I am aware of the offense and am remorseful. While the apology is not an instant salve, with time (like the old saying goes) there may now be a pathway to forgiveness and restoration."

Pride mutes apology and is callous to remorse. An unacknowledgment of harmful actions or words allows time to dig a deeper trench between individuals. Relationship reconciliation cannot happen without the admission of guilt and responsibility.

BUILD UP

Relationship reconciliation and strengthening more easily occur when we really know what makes the other person feels loved. "My child's love language is words of affirmation. I am not particularly strong in this area. I would love to have a list or some examples to study and practice." Amy wanted to be able to bless her daughter's heart by speaking her language. Of the five love expressions (words of affirmation, physical touch, gifts, acts of service, and quality time), words were what her daughter craved. This sensitive mom knows herself and her daughter well. She is willing to learn a second love language so she can demonstrate a deeper love to her daughter in the way she best receives it. She desires to parent to her daughter's uniqueness.

God calls us to train up our kids in the way they should go, to parent to their uniqueness. So often we love in the way we need to be loved and parent the way we were parented. But like Amy, we are not stuck. We can learn another way. We can become a student of our child, raising him or her in a way that best suits their personality, temperament, age, and stage.

Following Amy's request to be better able to speak directly to her daughter's need for words of affirmation, I created "101 Affirmations to Bless Your Child's Heart" (see appendix, page 167).

Affirmations are declarations of truth. They may be related to a relationship, a skill set, an observable character trait, or a promise of God. When articulating affirmation, be truthful, sincere, and specific. Kids have an acute sense of smell. They can sniff out a phony a mile away.

Following are ten affirmation declarations to get you started. These statements can be spoken, written, or texted to your little one or your young adult.

I like you.

I like the person you are becoming.

I love spending time with you. Would you like to come with me when I [fill in the blank]?

I appreciate your willingness to [fill in the blank].

I love your sense of humor.

I have confidence in your ability to figure this out.

I appreciate your respectful attitude.

God rejoices over you (Zephaniah 3:17).

God will help you (Isaiah 44:2).

God will never leave you (Hebrews 13:5).

Affirmations are a critical component of creating a connected family. By building the individual, we build up the family.

DEFEAT SHAME

It is no problem for me to build up my kids. When it comes to building myself up, I have trouble receiving affirmations. I sabotage compliments with deflection and negative self-talk. I am guilty of me-shaming. I say things like:

"I am *so* fat."

"I need to (eat less, exercise more, go on a diet, etc.)."

"I am such an idiot."

I would never talk to another human the way in which I speak to myself. The worst thing is, I don't keep my self-talk to myself. I verbalize it at home. It's time I set a guard over my mouth. (I was going to say big, fat mouth but thought better of it.) Shame is contagious.

Constant and consistent negative self-messaging impacts our children's belief about their self-worth and affects mood and behavior and has been linked to feelings of general anxiety. Fear is often the catalyst to self-destructive talk—fear of failure and fear of acceptance. Shame can manifest itself in substance abuse, broken relationships, cutting, anxiety, and eating disorders.

No parent wants to hear their child say, "I am so stupid." (Even though we may say these things about ourselves.) Often we rush in to fix it saying, "No, you are *so* smart." The attempt to fix it or to be overly optimistic may actually increase the negativity. The child may feel the need to convince mom or dad to see things the same way. At the very least, trying to make things better only pacifies the situation and doesn't deal with the root of the issue. Your child wants to be heard. When a child is experiencing an underlying problem, it needs to be addressed.

Reflect back to your child what you see and name the emotion, "Wow, I can see you are frustrated." Normalize the struggle. "Most people struggle with one thing or another. It's OK; that's how we learn." Empathize. Your kids need to know you struggle too. Challenge the self-talk by asking some questions to get a handle on the scope of the struggle. "Is it this particular assignment that is exasperating you?" Reframe the comment by helping your child say, "This assignment is frustrating," rather than, "I'm so stupid." Adjust the perspective by restating, "I feel so dumb when I have trouble with math." Rather than, "I am so stupid." Play a supportive role. Don't take over. Ask questions instead, like, "What's your plan?" or "How can I help?"

I am my own worst critic. My daughter Courtney scolds me for this habit, "Mom, that's not true. Don't say that about yourself." She is an encourager. It warms my heart that she attempts to protect me from myself. Her words remind me I must watch mine.

My kids need me to model healthy and realistic self-talk. It's important for their mental and emotional health for me to show I'm OK with my flaws and failures and comfortable with my strengths and successes. When I have a realistic view of myself, I will positively impact my children's view of themselves. When someone gives a compliment, it should be received with a thank you instead of being dismissed or deflected.

I'm learning, along with my parent coaching clients, how to receive a compliment. During small group sessions, we sometimes go around the group and encourage an individual who shared something he or she learned or celebrate a relationship victory. Often the response to that encouragement is, "I receive that. Thank you." To give encouragement feels natural, to receive it takes practice.

Scripture can increase our self-worth if we believe God when He says in Psalm 139:14a that we are fearfully and wonderfully made. In 1 Samuel 16:7, the Lord says He "does not look at the things people look at. People look at the outward appearance, but the LORD looks at the heart."

God loves us because He created us. He loves us for who we are not for what we do or how we look. Sherri Crandall, mom and vice president of global ministries and leadership at MOPS International, says in her post, "Identity Theft," for my blog: "God says that you are a masterpiece, created anew in Christ Jesus. You have been created in His image."

We are created on purpose, fully known and fully loved, and made in His image. These three messages stir confidence and provide a sense of purpose and hope. Even so, there are times our kids may struggle with self-talk. So as moms and dads, let's stop our negative comments and speak truth. Let's ask, "Who does God say I am?"

On 1corinthians13parenting.com, pastor, blogger, and dad J. L. Martin wrote, "We need to teach our children who God says they are from His Word. The Apostle Paul tells the church in Ephesus who they are before he tells them what to do. Every night at bedtime with all four of my kids, I remind them who they are in Christ . . . 'You are blessed, chosen, holy, blameless, loved, adopted, redeemed, forgiven, an inheritance, sealed by the Holy Spirit, fearfully and wonderfully made, and gifted. Use your gifts to glorify of God. May you grow in wisdom and stature and in favor with God and men. Amen.'"

Tom and I did not speak an identity blessing over our four when they all lived under our roof. I wish we had. Our oldest daughter has struggled all her life with her identity. I feel a bit guilty and partially responsible for her struggle. I wonder if she would have struggled a bit less if I had said a blessing like J. L.'s over her every night when she was younger. I realize some of her struggle comes from the abandonment she experienced as a baby. We adopted Courtney from Bogota, Colombia, when she was three months old. When she was in her later teens and early twenties, I put sticky notes on her mirror for her to read aloud: *I am a daughter of the King. I am fearfully and wonderfully made. I am precious in God's sight.* I thought my love and her dad's love for her would cure the pain of abandonment. I have realized the hole in her heart can only be filled by God and by fully believing who she is in Christ.

In a world fixated on image and reputation, both generated from another human's view, it is critical for kids to know how God sees them and that their life is important to God and the family. After all, God created us in His image!

Shame separates us from our identity in Christ. That can be changed when we connect with God, His Word, and what He says about us. Our identity is to be based on who God says we are. And He says we are His children.

COMMIT TO CONNECT

Interdependent connected families are united in identity and purpose and are motivated by personal investment and commitment. God gave Nehemiah this very wisdom when Jerusalem's walls needed to be swiftly rebuilt in order to protect and secure the city. The people were collectively and personally motivated to rebuild the wall. Each individual worked on and was responsible for the section of the wall closest to his own home (Nehemiah 3). The wall was up in fifty-two days, less than two months' time. The wall was such an amazing accomplishment that Jerusalem's enemies lost confidence. They realized that task could only have been completed so quickly with God's help (Nehemiah 6:15–16).

Nehemiah, with God's wisdom, knew how to compel the people to get that wall built. All the men had a vested interest in the wall going up efficiently and being effectively constructed. Each individual had skin in the game. The protection message resonated with the folks. Nehemiah spoke their language.

When we know our kids well, we can speak messages that resonate with them, just like Nehemiah did. The attitude of, "We are in this together," articulated by, "I'll help you clean it up," combined with the knowledge that each person is an important part of the solution creates the mindset of interdependency.

GET HAPPY

Doesn't it feel good to complete a task and check off the items on a never-ending to-do list? I wonder if the citizens of Jerusalem celebrated on day fifty-three. God created us to feel all kinds of emotions. It is through the emotional heartstrings that connections are tightly tied.

Joy and happiness are favorite feelings. My friend, Kathy Wolfe, tells how treasuring the state of joyfulness caused her to pray. "When I was in college, I prayed for a husband who first had a good sense of humor and second who loved the Lord. Maybe I should have reversed the order. But God wasn't put off by my prayer. He knew my heart. He blessed me with Chris, a fun-loving and funny guy with a big faith."

We love to laugh; we enjoy joy. And God created happiness. Neuroscientists confirm that our brains positively respond to things that make us happy. Alex Korb, UCLA neuroscience researcher and author of *The Upward Spiral: Using Neuroscience to Reverse the Course of Depression, One Small Change at a Time*, has given us four ways to tap into and increase our happy meter. They include gratefulness, feeling identification, decision-making, and giving and receiving affection. I've taken Dr. Korb's ideas and applied them to parenting.

Train your children to ask, "What am I grateful for?"

Focus on thankfulness and gratitude to increase happiness. A prayer was given prior to me speaking at a moms' event, "Lord, thank You that the dog threw up on the hardwood floor and not the carpet this morning." As this leader prayed, we laughed. A thankful heart plus a good sense of humor is contagious.

When a person expresses appreciation, often those around him or her catch the joy wave. Scientifically speaking, we laughed because her gratefulness boosted our brains' neurotransmitters, dopamine, and serotonin. Help your kiddos get happy by encouraging a grateful and thankful outlook.

Teach your children to name their feelings.

In those times children are really down in the dumps, encourage them to label their emotions. As parents, we are in a position to help our kids out, "You appear frustrated." "You must be feeling really sad right now." The really little ones can begin by naming their emotions four ways: glad, sad, mad, and scared. By identifying how one feels rather than ignoring or suppressing the pain, the brain is more able to deal with the issue.

Encourage your children to make a decision.

Rather than fuss over a decision until it's perfect or procrastinate making a choice, be decisive. Worry and anxiety are caused when a decision is delayed. Once a decision is made our brain feels at rest and relaxed. Train your children in setting goals, finding solutions, and solving problems. Have them create a list and check off things that have been completed. These activities actually calm the limbic system and increase pleasure.

Show, give, and receive affection.
Touch increases our happiness and lessens our physical pain. Intuitively we know this. That is why we hold a loved one's hand when they are getting a shot or in some type of pain. Research shows that five hugs a day for four weeks significantly increases happiness. Scientifically speaking, big bear hugs are much better than the quick, stiff, obligatory hug.

Our brain chemically responds to these four things. Serotonin and dopamine increase (the happy chemicals) and cortisol (the stress hormone) decreases. If we want happy kids let's train them to be grateful, identify their emotions, make good decisions, and give and receive hugs. be affectionate

> Is anyone among you in trouble? Let them pray. Is anyone
> happy? Let them sing songs of praise. —James 5:13

FACE THE FEAR FACTOR

We all want our kids to be happy. What parent doesn't? How many times have we heard or said, "I just want my child to be happy"? Happiness is a part of our collective human experience. Happiness, along with anger, sadness, and fear, is one of our basic emotions. We need all four. Happiness brings joy and laughter. Anger can move us to acts of justice or peace making. Sadness births empathy and compassion while fear draws out courage and bravery. God even tells us in Romans 12:15 to, "Rejoice with those who rejoice; mourn with those who mourn." We are to respond to others according to their emotional state.

It is pretty easy to connect on the happiness level. But that leaves three other basic human emotions. Our kiddos won't have a life that is only one-fourth lived. They will experience anger, sadness, and fear. Chapters 4 and 7 fully cover ways to connect and foster interdependence during conflict and grief. In this section, we will dissect the fear factor.

When we sense fear and have a friend near, we instinctively reach for and cling to that person. It was my friend Darcy's birthday. To celebrate we decided to go through the seven-acre corn maze at Chatfield Farms. We are both directionally challenged, so the seven acres of winding through corn stalks was above our pay grade. We veered off the maze path a bit. Yes, we cheated. Don't judge us because we would still be there if we hadn't.

Anyway, as we made our own trail through the corn toward the exit, we heard some rustling. We jumped, screamed a little, grabbed each other's hand, and bolted. A couple birds flew out with us. We convinced one another it was most likely the sparrows responsible for the noise, but . . . it could have been a giant rat. One never knows.

That sort of scary fear can be fun. My four kids love to go with me on roller coasters because I'm the fraidy-cat, and they are the fearless ones.

Real fear bonds us together and summons bravery. Every summer when I was growing up, my parents, brother, sister, and I spent time on Rabbit Lake at the family cabin in Aitkin, Minnesota. One Saturday evening a big storm kicked up. Sheets of water flew across the lake and splashed onto the big bay window in the family room. My dad flipped on the radio. A tornado was headed our way. The sky was black and the lake churned. The five of us huddled together on the other side of a flimsy wooden plank wall. My siblings, Todd and Keri, huddled with me in the center of the family circle while our parents tightly wrapped their arms around us. We felt scared and safe all at the same time. We knew our parents would protect us.

Fear faced builds character; it provides opportunities to demonstrate courage. Fear can also build trust.

We want to give our kids the message that no matter what scary thing is around the corner, dad and mom won't run away, instead we will wrap our arms around them. We will be with them in the storm. They are safe.

INTERDEPENDENT INTIMACY

While raising kids, a lot of time is spent dealing with the here and now, troubleshooting unacceptable behaviors. Of course parents need to address inappropriate actions and train for acceptable and appropriate behavior. Perhaps that is why the natural and logical consequence approach to parenting is so popular. We are simply distracted, so we deal with the things that catch our attention. The result of putting out the fire still leaves some smoldering ashes. A single focus on the smoke rather than the reason for the hot coals never gets to why the fires started in the first place. Seek the why in order to develop the child's internal character.

When character development occurs, family ties are strengthened. Sadly, I have observed the culture of raising independent kids is stomping all over our natural desire and longing for strong families.

We want a fast fix. The culture of busyness and competition combined with either too much or too little parent control or one that's too child-centric affects how parents and kids relate to and connect with one another.

While reading through 1 Samuel 18—20, I noticed certain qualities in both David and Jonathan that set the stage for a powerful interdependent connection and godly friendship. They had a bond of faith, an emotional attachment, were committed to each other, and had a mutual respect (1 Samuel 18:1–4). Jonathan even sacrificed for David by giving David his robe and military garb. This signified Jonathan, who was King Saul's son and a natural heir to the throne, understood that David would be Saul's successor not him. In 1 Samuel 19:1–7, we see Jonathan's loyalty and concern for David. Jonathan even stood up for his friend and rebuked his own father. The two friends were able to talk over hard things and listen to one another (1 Samuel 20).

Reinforce and train for the characteristics like the ones David and Jonathan exhibited in 1 Samuel to have an interdependent, connected family. Intimacy within the family structure can be built with the five factors of trust, honesty, encouragement, humility, and availability.

There will be no connection or personal growth if there is no trust. Trust is built in a family when we treat each other with respect, hold confidence, and do what we say we will. Accountability, responsibility, responsiveness to needs, and integrity are building blocks of trust.

Honesty occurs when trust is in place. When we value and model a respectful expression of honest emotions and are clear about our own strengths and weaknesses, our children will have permission to be human—flawed yet able to flourish. They will develop confidence in who they are and who they can become. We want to avoid the message that only certain opinions, feelings, or skills are acceptable in family. If we are OK with respectful freedom of expression and thought, unconditional love is lived out. We don't want to train our kids to be chameleons who become who they think they need to be to suit the situation in order to gain acceptance. And while honesty is important, it isn't carte blanche to be insensitive and blunt. Any conversation that starts with, "I'm not going to lie . . ." comes with a red flag.

Cold and insensitive honesty creates relational barriers while encouragement knocks down walls. "You can do it," or, "I'm here if you need me," are statements that draw people together. "It's your problem; you deal with it," pulls people apart. The role of encourager empowers others.

When one has an honest assessment of personal strengths and weaknesses, humility forms. It is not low self-esteem but rather a realistic view of who one is and who others are. Humility is characterized by thinking more about the other guy than oneself. Jonathan showed great humility when he offered his robe and gear to David. Jonathan realized it was God's will for David to be the future king rather than himself, the expected successor.

Humility allows us to support another's endeavors without envy or jealousy. It provides a safe place for personal thoughts, dreams, hopes, disappointments, and fears. Vulnerable conversations shutdown when we teach our kids to be guarded, protective, and suspicious. Humility doesn't mean everything is aired without a filter. Wisdom in how much to share and discernment with whom to share is called for.

Emotional availability—to be present, real, and accessible—is birthed from humility. Empathy and compassion for another's struggle cements relationships. Because an emotionally present person realizes life is not all about him, he is able to actively listen, acutely observe, and demonstrate compassion. He is attentive, connected, and tuned in. People flock to this type of person because they feel understood and cared for in his presence.

To have an interdependent connected family the characteristics of encouragement, honesty, humility, trustworthiness, and emotional availability can be developed in ourselves and in our children. When those attributes are valued in the individual they will spill over into family relationships, creating a connected environment. Add David and Jonathan's common bond of faith, emotional attachment, commitment, sacrifice, respect, and good communication skills, and we are sure to have a family that is connected and united.

> *Let the peace of Christ rule in your hearts, since as members of one body you were called to peace. And be thankful. Let the message of Christ dwell among you richly as you teach and admonish one another with all wisdom through psalms, hymns, and songs from the Spirit, singing to God with gratitude in your hearts. And whatever you do, whether in word or deed, do it all in the name of the Lord Jesus, giving thanks to God the Father through him. —Colossians 3:15–17*

CHAPTER 3

MESSAGES THAT BOND

I myself am convinced, my brothers and sisters, that you yourselves are full of goodness, filled with knowledge and competent to instruct one another.
—Romans 15:14

One snowy winter evening, Tom and I got a frantic call from our twentysomething daughter, Courtney, as she was leaving work.

"I went to brush the snow off my windshield and the wiper popped off."

Wipers are a critical component when driving through the sheets of white blowing in the Colorado wind. My mama's heart wanted to run to her, to rescue her from this dilemma. I pictured Tom reinserting the wiper while I consoled my child. Tom could be Hero Dad and I could be Mother Nurturer. (Are you like me? Do you first react to the feelings then later respond with your brain?)

Then God popped a different vision into my head. I saw Courtney fix the wiper herself and then smile with pride in her ability to handle her issue.

"What is best for her? Do we help her out or help her up?" With the eyes God gave me, I didn't have to ponder this long.

"You are mechanically minded. There is an owner's manual in the glove compartment. Read it and follow the directions. You are fully capable to do this job. Dad and I have full confidence in you and your ability."

As I hung up the phone, I turned to my husband and said, "There is no way she's going to be able to do this." Thankfully I kept my fear silent from Courtney's ears. She heard what she needed to hear.

My daughter was empowered to manage her situation. Our stated belief in her capability fueled her confidence. The phone rang ten minutes later, "I did it. I am on my way back home!" The joy of accomplishment she felt once the wiper was secured was priceless. If we had jumped in to save the day due to our own worry, we would have robbed her of that experience.

EMPOWERING MESSAGES

"I will never forget my husband's words when I told him about a struggle I was having. Rather than giving me a solution to my problem, he listened. He steadied his gazed and stated, 'You are a smart woman. I know you will be able to manage this well.'"

Michelle went on to say, "I have forgotten the details of the particular issue now, but I have not forgotten my husband's words. His certainty in my ability was so empowering; it made all the difference. I was able to tackle the difficulty with confidence."

A mom requested I write an article that included empowering statements parents could say to their kids. She wanted sound bites that could be displayed on the refrigerator or on the child's bathroom mirror. Here are fifteen empowering verses and three powerful messages you can verbalize or prominently post no matter the age of your child:

When your child lacks confidence:
You are able (Philippians 4:13).
You are capable (Philippians 4:13).
God has equipped you (2 Timothy 3:16–17).
God created you for a purpose (Psalm 138:8; 139:16).
"I have every confidence that you are able and capable because God has equipped you and created you for a purpose."

When your child feels unlovable or rejected:
You are the apple of God's eye (Zechariah 2:8).
God accepts you (Ephesians 1:6).
You are God's child (John 1:12).

God cherishes you (Ephesian 2:4).

You are loved (John 3:16).

You are valuable (Luke 12:24).

"You are loved and valuable to God. The Cross shows you how much."

When your child is fearful:

God is with you (Psalm 73:23).

God will give you courage (Psalm 46:1–2).

God calls you a conqueror (Romans 8:37).

God guards you (2 Timothy 1:12).

God is your power (Ephesians 3:20; Philippians 3:12).

"You can tackle your fear because God is with you. He has given you a spirit of power and strength."

"God is with you." Those were the words I spoke to my unconscious daughter as she was whisked away to emergency surgery. Kendra and I had rushed to St. Anthony's hospital via ambulance. The emergency medical team stood outside the hospital doors waiting for us to arrive. They wasted no time and began to prep her even as she was wheeled into the building. My sixteen-year-old had been injured in a snowboard accident.

The trauma nurse furrowed her brow and steadied her eyes in my direction, "Sometimes life doesn't turn out the way we want it to."

I guess she thought I didn't understand the severity of Kendra's accident. But I definitely did. Still I wondered if I had said the right thing to Kendra. I deflected the nurse's comment and focused on God, "Lord, what in the world? The last thing I say to my child is, 'God is with you'? I should have said, 'I love you.'"

God instantly pressed into my mind, "No; she knows that. She needs to know I am with her."

Kendra had ruptured her spleen. God was indeed with us—with her, as He always is and will be. A few days later, while Kendra recovered in the trauma ICU, I asked her if she heard my words before she went into surgery, "Yes, you said God is with you." Then as if on cue, a voice boomed over the hospital loud speaker, "So do not fear, for I am with you; do not be dismayed, for I am your God. I will strengthen you and help you; I will uphold you with my righteous right hand" (Isaiah 41:10).

God spoke loud and clear. He was with my daughter and wanted her to know. Our kiddos need the message that they are loved, lovable, capable, and most importantly God is always with them.

Our God is a God in whom we can fully depend. We can help our children develop a God dependence through trusting Him in hard places. We can empower them with the assurance that the Lord is with them when they struggle or suffer when we speak words blended with love, grace, and His truth.

CORRECTION NOT CRITICISM

Relationships are strengthened and correction is more easily received when words are bathed in love, grace, and truth.

"Correction is not rejection." I was speaking to a group of women about effectively training kids for good behavior while encouraging character development.

One mom raised her hand in response to my comment on correction and stated, "Whenever I try and correct my four-year-old daughter she says, 'Mommy, that hurts my heart.'"

This tender mom worried about hurting her clever little one's heart and felt reluctant to correct her.

"Why don't you try this? Tell her you are not speaking to her heart, you are talking to her head."

Everyone laughed, including me. God spoke right through me in that moment. I am never that smart or clever. In fact I was so surprised with what came out of my mouth, I asked the moms to write it down for me. I didn't want to forget that great response.

Correction addresses the mind and is a part of interdependency. The way correction is received is an indication of the heart. Children don't come straight out of the shoot knowing the best way to act. In fact, if left to their own devices, many kids guess wrong. Parents are God's tools to correct and train children (Proverbs 15:31–32).

Growth typically comes by being stretched, challenged, corrected, and then convicted. Correction doesn't sound like sarcasm or criticism. Sarcasm and criticism create an independent, embittered, and rebellious spirit in the receiver. If we want to have interdependent families, we use techniques that bring us together rather than separate us. The idea of everybody spills takes the sting out of the training. Humility softens the heart and opens the ear to correction.

DEFENSIVE OR RECEPTIVE

Peter, post denial, is a good example of how to receive correction. In Acts 10, he had a vision. While he was thinking about the vision, the Spirit told him to go with three men who were to take him to Cornelius the centurion's home. Peter began to understand the message in his vision—the Lord had removed the barrier between Jew and Gentile and all men should hear the message of Jesus Christ.

Despite God's message in the vision, Peter later began to feel peer pressure and stopped eating meals with the Gentiles. Instead he ate separately with the Jews (Galatians 2). Paul noticed this and corrected (maybe *confronted* is a better word) Peter about his behavior, both personally and publicly (vv. 11 and 14). Who Peter dined with was a big deal. His actions were motivated by fear of the Jews, caused others to stumble, were hypocritical, and went against the message of the gospel (vv. 12–14). Peter received Paul's correction well. It was clear, specific, and not personal. Paul was right. Peter was wrong. Peter was convicted and adjusted his actions accordingly. These two leaders were committed to the same mission. Correction is a readjustment not rejection.

POISONOUS PRAISE

Learning is generated by failure more than it is by success. So why are we afraid to let our kids know they are imperfect? Do we worry we will break their spirit or hurt their heart by training them?

Dr. Jim Dempsey, author of *Parenting Unchained*, tackled this very subject in a blog titled, "Too Much Praise Can Be Poisonous."

"We give all participants awards so no one feels unsuccessful. We care so much about self-esteem that we create a false sense of importance within our children. What's so bad about focusing on self-esteem? When we inflate self-esteem, we cause problems in several areas of life.

"First, none of us likes to be around someone who has an inflated view of himself. An arrogant boss likely won't value your input. If Mr. Bighead works for you, he probably won't take direction well.

"An arrogant person cares more about himself than others. As self-centered people climb the corporate ladder, they often see others as rungs.

"But did you know that too much praise can actually keep your child off the ladder to success? Children who are drenched in the wrong kind of praise grow up lacking two essential qualities for success.

"Kids hooked on praise lack the confidence to fail. Children praised for being wonderful develop a perverse fear of failure, not wanting to risk failing. In a recent study, researchers gave the same test to two groups of kids. Regardless of their scores, the first group was praised for being smart. The second group was praised for effort.

"Among the students praised for effort, 90 percent subsequently chose to take a harder test when offered. But the majority of the students praised for being smart chose to take an easier test. Apparently these 'smart' kids couldn't risk losing their lofty position so they opted to avoid the harder challenge. When children are willing to risk failure, they discover a key to success.

"Kids inundated with praise lack the willingness to persevere. Children who must protect their reputations rarely perceive failure as an invitation to try again. These kids are scared to fail, so they only seek out challenges they can master. They quit in the face of a hard task.

"When you must praise, do so for effort. Simply express an interest in what your children are doing. Instead of praising, ask them to tell you about what they're working on.

"If you lie and tell a child he's a prodigy when he's not, you lose credibility and any praise provided loses its value. If you want your child to seek out challenges and develop internal motivation, hold off on poisonous praise."

Our kids will be better equipped to succeed if they develop the skills of perseverance and endurance rather than receive false and abundant praise. The ability to be comfortable with the risk of failure and then to apply grit are the secret ingredients to our children's success. Flattery is insincere and manipulative, and kids know it. Proverbs 29:5 speaks to the motivation for flattery.

> *A man who flatters his neighbor is spreading a net for his steps. —Proverbs 29:5 NASB*

A SAFE HOUSE

It was once thought that telling our kid they are smart was a way to increase self-esteem, thereby increasing their ability to learn. Common sense and studies prove we need to tell children two things: (1) they have God-given gifts and abilities, but that doesn't mean everything will be easy; and (2) effort, creativity, and perseverance are a few of the necessary character qualities to achieve success.

Praise is good if it is specific and true—like giving an acknowledgement of success via congratulations for a particular accomplishment. Of course, celebrate. But to insincerely tell kids they are the best, the brightest, and the most talented will backfire. Scripture tells us to have an accurate view of ourselves, "Do not think of yourself more highly than you ought, but rather think of yourself with sober judgment, in accordance with the faith God has distributed to each of you" (Romans 12:3).

Creativity is bred through discovering ways to solve a problem. Failure is part of the creative experience. The ability to push through the frustration with the determination to figure out a solution fosters the "I'm not giving up" mentality. Moments of struggle or a challenge increase personal potential. The hope given through sincere praise regarding the child's abilities combined with the motivation to persevere is powerful. Confidence plus exertion will give them what they need to move through the frustration to find success.

For our kids to receive correction, believe affirmation, or confide in us, they need to feel secure and believe we are sincere. It's up to mom and dad to create an emotionally safe home.

"How do we make our kids feel like they can come to us with serious problems?" This is a real question asked by a dad in one of my parenting classes. My short answer is, "We don't." We can't make our kids come to us with their problems, big or small. We can create an environment where they feel comfortable coming to us with a struggle.

Begin with our Spillage Parenting Philosophy catch phrase: "That's OK, everybody [fill in the blank]. I'll help you clean it up." We lay the groundwork for handling problems in a positive way while keeping the relationship intact. If we freak out over the spills, we have shown our kids we are not safe to come to when things go badly or a mess is made.

To assess if our home is a safe haven for our kids, we need to do some self-examination. I do this assessment when I speak to a group of parents. I hope to raise the bar rather than smack the audience with shame. I begin by having the moms and dads repeat a few statement. We start with: "I am not a perfect parent."

They laugh. That's easy to say. No one thinks they are the perfect parent.

The next statement is tougher. I have them speak to the people on either side of them and say, "And you are not a perfect parent either." There is a small amount of resistance to this. But my purpose is understood. We tend to compare our parenting to another's, thinking everyone else does it better. The fact is everyone struggles.

Finally I have them point at me and say, "She's not a perfect parent either."

I reassure them I am not Mary Poppins. Parenting is a series of trials and successes for everyone.

OK, now that the playing field is leveled, we can go ahead and evaluate where we can do better.

Am I trustworthy with confidential information?

"When I was twelve, I told my mom who I had a crush on. I asked her not to tell. She told her friends and they asked me about it. They were laughing. I was embarrassed. I think that was one of my most humiliating moments. That incident created a wedge between my mom and me even to this day," a young mom confided in me at a speaking event. Her confidential information had been shared and that caused relational damage.

Am I sensitive to personal struggles and hopes shared?

As parents we have a front row seat to our kid's victories and defeats. We must hold this information tenderly. Personal moments may include: struggling with a subject in school, being accepted at a certain university, or even potty training.

Difficult moments can create a need for some empathy and support. The phone is often the vehicle to find a sympathetic ear. Our cells are attached to our bodies while our kids are Velcroed to our legs. Every word, every tone is heard by those little ears. Just because our kids are short, doesn't mean their ears don't hear things above their head. This is an example of being insensitive to struggles and untrustworthy with confidential information. We want our kids to know we are a vault that will keep their personal struggles under lock and key. This builds trust in the family system.

Do I refrain from using personal information as a weapon later?

Avoid being the parent who is a historian and brings up issues from the past. Know your children's personal temptations and weaknesses to help steer and guide them rather than use that information to hurt or shame them.

Am I able to handle the small irritations and inconveniences in life with calm and patience?

This is hard for us all. It helps to have a response to regain composure. Repeat, "That's OK, everybody spills. I'll help you clean it up." Hopefully by the time you say the third line your teeth will unclench.

Do I remain calm when bad decisions are made or accidents occur?

My answer is no, not always. Tom is much better at handling the bigger life spills. He helps me with this. To get over the hump of annoyance or even anger, try and recall that these are opportunities for learning. And remember who you were and things you did at the same age.

Do I avoid comparing my child to his or her siblings or peers?

Sometimes our good intentions don't create the best results. Comparing kids is not motivational to the child who needs to up his or her game. This might sound like, "See how often your brother practices? That is why he is doing so well at pitching. If you practice as much, you will do better too." Be careful or you will unintentionally set the stage for sibling rivalry.

Am I able to deal directly with a problem rather than use a passive aggressive approach?

Saying, "I'm just kidding," "Fine, whatever," "Are you nuts?" or ignoring, threatening, procrastinating, and keeping score are all ways parents can be passive aggressive.

Can I be kind even when I disagree?

We can disagree agreeably. This is a skill. Kindness bids us to stick to the topic and avoid personal attacks. Listen. Ask questions. Attempt to understand a new point of view. Consider each one's position.

Do I let my children express their opinions and thoughts even if they are different from mine?

Leave room for respectful dialogue. Our kids need to know their parents are not threatened by differing points of view and opinions. We can disagree and discuss respectfully. We learn about our kids and who they are becoming by giving them the freedom to discuss and articulate their point of view.

Am I real with my kids? Do I let them know I experience struggles and make mistakes?

Parents who admit to imperfection are more approachable. Kids need to know mom and dad are human too.

Are my expectations realistic or perfection-based?

Kids are imperfect beings, just as parents are. No one is great at everything. Really, everybody does spill.

Is my home a place where it is OK to be less than perfect and a little weird sometimes?

At three years old, my son wore buckets on his head. Not just one but a stack. Jake went to preschool, church, and everywhere else with his buckets on his head. He's twenty-seven now and doesn't wear buckets anymore. Jaime, his wife, can vouch for this. Let your kids be a little weird.

After some honest self-examination, make the necessary adjustments. We can all do better. When our homes are built on respect, empathy, understanding, loyalty, trust, humility, grace, and unconditional love, we create an atmosphere where our children will share their struggles both big and small. We can't make them tell us their problems. We can do something better. We can foster a relationship where they want to invite us into their lives, telling us about their struggles and successes.

To answer before listening—that is folly and shame.
—Proverbs 18:13

PURPOSE SPURS CONFIDENCE

"Are you someone important?" How would you respond to this highly unusual question from a total stranger?

I was flying to Alabama for a Transformation Ministries event where I was to be the keynote speaker and workshop presenter for the next three days. From Dallas to Birmingham, the second leg of the flight, I was seated next to an older couple who wanted to know why I was going to Alabama. Rather than simply ask why I was headed to where the Camellia blooms, the gentleman inquired if I was important.

"My husband thinks I am," was my weak reply. I wish I had confidently answered, "Yes, I am. I have been created on purpose for a purpose. Just like you."

Confidence is birthed when our kids believe their life matters. Life with purpose is a life that makes a difference. Most kids today want to make a contribution and positive impact on the world around them. In an article for entrepreneur.com titled "Why a Purpose-Driven Mission Is Key to Motivating Millennials," author Ahmad Raza states, "The millennial generation is all about being part of a greater purpose." Being part of a grander design brings focus and hope.

When a young person believes his or her life doesn't matter, they may start to experience feelings of futility and hopelessness. If he or she thinks their life is a cosmic accident, then life has no meaning. Lack of purpose can lead to feeling hopeless. Depression combined with hopelessness can trigger suicide. Behind accidents, suicide is the leading cause of death among teens and young adults.

Our kids are literally dying to know they are important. They need to believe their life matters, that they are created on purpose for a purpose.

There is a current parenting trend to let children develop (or to not develop) faith on their own. These parents intentionally choose not to educate children about spiritual or religious things or, conversely, they present a smorgasbord of concepts and allow their children pick what suits them best. Ultimately, this puts the child in God's place.

"Secular parents are by no means a cohesive unit; our struggles are hardly singular," says Wendy Thomas Russell in her article "10 Commandments for talking to your kids about religion" for PBS Newshour. "But most of us—whether we consider ourselves atheist, agnostic, humanist, deist, or nothing at all—do share a common goal: To raise kind, happy, tolerant kids capable of making up their own minds about what to believe."

Yet these same parents will help their children learn science and math concepts and teach them how to read and write. In Deuteronomy 6:4–9, God tells us to talk about things of faith when we rise, in our comings and goings, and when we lay down to sleep. God wants to be known. He wants to have a relationship with us and with our kids.

If our children believe in a Creator rather than a random big bang, they will be able to grasp the concept that they are created on purpose. And if they believe they are created for a purpose, that purpose will involve other people. The knowledge that life is created intentionally encourages God dependence and interpersonal interdependence among God's people.

The Lord has a good purpose for your child. Help him or her discover God's design for their life. They need to know they are loved and loveable, capable, and created purposefully for a purpose. When our children believe God is with them and God created them on purpose, for a purpose, they will be motivated and empowered to move forward.

May these words of my mouth and this meditation of my heart be pleasing in your sight, LORD, my Rock and my Redeemer. —Psalm 19:14

CHAPTER 4

CONFLICT DOESN'T MEAN SEPARATION

Be kind and compassionate to one another, forgiving each other, just as in Christ God forgave you.
—Ephesians 4:32

One summer we attended a family reunion in Holden Beach, North Carolina. There were nine families represented. The house burst at the seams with little kids, teens, college kids, parents, and grandparents. Adult conversation overtook the upstairs family room while the recreation room, a floor below, was the third generation's hang out.

One evening in the upper room, the topic of faith was broached. Those participating in the discussion were an agnostic, an atheist, and a couple believers. The dialogue was so full of energy that my seventy-five-year-old mother-in-law put a stop to it. She scolded her fifty-year-old son and the rest of the "boys." Even though the people involved were all comfortable with the spirited conversation, those of us on the periphery of the debate felt uncomfortable.

Many of my husband's family members are at ease stating opposing opinions and beliefs. They are not at all troubled when conversations get intense. They don't shy away from hot topics. In fact, they press into them.

This type of conversation isn't my idea of a good time. I experience discomfort when a debate gets rolling. Yet it is a great example of how to present various points of view while keeping the relationship intact. A disagreement on principles does not mean lack of acceptance of a person. Often we don't see eye-to-eye with those we live with and love.

Words can draw us together or they can divide. What we say and how we say it makes a difference. If we truly want to connect with each other on a healthy interdependent level we should be able to talk about the taboo topics of politics, religion, ethics, and money without the fear of relational disintegration.

When watching a political debate, it is clear there is little regard for the relationship. The focus of the forum is to win. Sarcasm, name-calling, interruption, talking over, lack of listening, and domination are all ways one can be heard, but it comes at a cost. An intact relationship may not matter in the political arena, but in the family a damaged or broken relationship is a high price to pay.

Respect is the missing ingredient in many political debates. Discussions based on respect for each person demonstrates the relationship is valued more than the issue being discussed.

ANTISOCIAL

Social media is not the place for our kids to learn how to discuss issues. Many apply a similar approach to that used by politicians—only worse. Internet "trolls" hide their identity but display cruel and condescending messages publicly. Others boldly and rudely speak their mind with the intent to offend and do harm. These people have never learned how to effectively communicate their point of view without using a personal attack. When this occurs it is totally OK to remove their comments, unfriend, or even block.

"I think you should block him," my sister once advised me as to how to respond to an individual who made negative and argumentative comments on my personal Facebook page.

Keri continued, "Let me ask you, why are you on Facebook?"

"For business and social reasons."

"Does this person's actions help or hurt those goals?"

"His comments are antagonistic, condescending, and divisive. He hurts my objective."

"What would you do if you didn't know this person?" Keri pressed further.

"I'd immediately block him."

"I think that's your answer."

My sister helped me clarify my purpose, goals, and desires. I have taken control of my social media by setting clear boundaries. Comments must be respectful or they will be removed.

BOUNDARIES

Boundaries are created from convictions and conscience. They are for the person setting them. They are not meant to encourage relational alienation. Interdependence isn't boundary free. It may allow for compromise or it may not.

Libby, a mom of an adult daughter, shares her experience with boundary setting. "My daughter and her live-in boyfriend were coming to visit. I struggled with how to approach the sleeping arrangements. *Is it ridiculous to separate them since they live together?* I decided it was important to me to maintain integrity by standing by my conviction that only married people should share a bed. I decided to let my daughter and her boyfriend know they were welcome to stay but they would need to sleep in separate quarters."

In an interdependent family or friend relationship, sometimes we don't agree. Interdependency doesn't equal unconditional support. It does mean unconditional love. Contrary to the notion the current culture professes, we don't have to agree in order to love one another. The principle and the person are not to be responded to in the same manner. We accept and love people; we agree or disagree on principles. In Luke 6:32, Jesus said, "If you love those who love you, what credit is that to you? Even sinners love those who love them."

It can be a little surprising and sometimes disconcerting for parents of young adults who have begun to formulate, articulate, and then act on their ideas. But it is possible to disagree on principles while still loving the people who hold thoughts, beliefs, and ideas different from our own. It is simple but it is not easy. Parents need to set the stage for healthy conversation.

DISCUSS OR DEBATE

The ability to discuss rather than debate requires the establishment of ground rules. Each person is entitled to his or her opinion and belief. Ridicule, sarcasm, and domineering are not allowed. To have a respectful exchange we must present convictions concisely using logic rather than emotion while avoiding longwinded lectures. Instead take turns, listen, then consider the other person's opinion. Try to seek common ground. Find the golden nugget where you can agree. In a close connected family it is to be expected that there will be opposing points of view. We can disagree agreeably.

Here are five rules of engagement for hot topics:

1. Know the facts.
2. Speak out of your head, not your emotions.
3. Always maintain respect.
4. Listen for understanding.
5. Avoid attempts to convince or coerce. (Those are debates, not discussions.)

If it is an impossible task to implement the five rules of engagement, it may be best to avoid hot topics like religion or politics. The way we speak and the words we say will echo in our kids' heads, just like our parents' voices are heard in ours.

GROW A CONSCIENCE

Differing points of views, beliefs, and experiences can create conflict. The knowledge of conscience development gives perspective on where the other person is coming from.

Our kids need parental help and supernatural intervention when it comes to growing a conscience. To keep the moral compass of the conscience functioning properly, the Holy Spirit must be involved.

Without the influence of the Holy Spirit, the conscience will fall back on emotions to dictate good and bad, right and wrong. The idea of, "It feels right so let's do it," or, "Let your heart tell you what to do," are statements of an underdeveloped conscience—one without the Holy Spirit. Sometimes, oftentimes, doing the right thing doesn't feel good and is typically inconvenient.

I have surmised there are six phases of conscience development. These phases shed light on how loved ones deal with conflict and resolve problems.

Phase 1: Infancy

"If it hurts, it's bad. If it feels good, it's good." (Being hungry is bad because it hurts.) With babies, this is the time to build trust by responding to their needs. If one is spiritually in the infant stage he may say, "Because it feels so good when I'm with you, I know it's OK to have sex with you." The conscience in this case is emotions-driven. It's right if it feels good.

Phase 2: Toddler

"Hitting is bad because I get into trouble." Behavior is good or bad depending on the consequence. With toddlers this is the time to establish acceptable and unacceptable behavior, rules, and consequences. An adult in the toddler stage of conscience development may say, "I won't have sex with you because I could get pregnant." This stage is obedience-driven. It's right if it follows the rule or the law.

Phase 3: Preschool to Seven Years Old

"It's wrong because my family doesn't do it that way." With this age group, this is the time to talk about "Team [last name]" and establish family unity and identity. The Golden Rule can be applied at this phase. This is the age of "Why" and the perfect time to begin in earnest talking about family values, morals, and faith. An adult at this spiritual phase may say, "I go to church because that is what people in my family do." (Those who have failed to connect bounce back to phase 2—the toddler phase—and say, "If I do it and don't get caught it's OK.") Conscience is tradition-driven. "It's right because that's how I was raised."

Phase 4: Intermediate Ages

"It's right if it's equal." At this stage kids realize mom and dad are not perfect. They are keenly aware of fairness. "That's not fair." With the intermediate age group this is a great time to say, "I'll do this, if you do that," establishing more family responsibility and reciprocity. Spiritually speaking, someone at this phase may say, "God, why does this happen to me when I do this for You?" Shoulds and shouldn'ts are evident in this person's vocabulary. A "What's in it for me," even-steven mentality. This stage is fairness-driven.

Phase 5: Preteen to Teen

"Kids my age always [fill in the blank]. That's what we do." People pleasing can also be a part of this phase. "I will do [fill in the blank] to be accepted." In this phase it is good to ask questions to get kids thinking so they can see if the decisions they are making are solid ones or are peer pressure driven. This stage is driven by the culture. It's right if the culture says it is.

Phase 6: Mature

"It's right because God says it's right." A healthy, mature moral compass is one where thinking, feeling, and acting with empathy and compassion lead a person to do the good and right thing—just because it is good and right. Right thinking, feeling, and action occur in spite of good or bad feelings, rules (laws), tradition, fairness, or society. This stage is driven by a higher power. God and His Word set the moral standard of right and wrong.

To reach phase six we must let our kids know they are unconditionally loved by us and by God. They need to embrace the truth that God's Word helps us all live well.

Empathy is fostered when kindness and respect are demonstrated in our homes and is a critical component of conscience development. When we listen to our kids, set limits, follow through with consequences, teach responsibility, not allow for aggressive talk or actions, and avoid rescuing them from sadness, discomfort, or failure, we can influence healthy conscience development.

When we train our kids to live for the Audience of One, they are free to make decisions that may be countercultural, which is a courageous thing to do. When they look to God rather than man they will be ready to hear His still small voice over the dull roar of the masses. By helping our kids grow a Holy Spirit-driven conscience they will be mature, wise, loving, and discerning people who honor God with their thoughts, words, and deeds.

My conscience confirms it through the Holy Spirit.
—Romans 9:1

THE THINKING MODE

Lots of parents steer clear of kid disagreements. Their intention is good. But "let the kids figure it out themselves" is a survival-of-the-fittest approach. Without proper training, the weaker or younger individual is metaphorically consumed by the older, stronger, or more cunning sibling.

We don't want to fall to the opposite extreme either, playing the role of judge or referee. When we insert ourselves into the equation we set the stage for triangulation, a situation where we become the third party to a conflict between two people. We need to train our kids to directly and constructively address conflict without mom and dad managing the disagreement or relationship.

The first thing to tackle is the emotions stirred by conflict. For kids to self-regulate they need to move out of the emotion-driven limbic system to the frontal lobe where the reasoning part of the brain is found.

We can help them learn to reason during frustrating sibling moments by reminding the older sibling of the younger one's age. Have the elder say to himself, "My brother is only [fill in the blank] years old." Give the older child some empathy for the younger one.

Scripture states, "When I was a child, I talked like a child, I thought like a child, I reasoned like a child. When I became a man, I put the ways of childhood behind me" (1 Corinthians 13:11). Children will act in childlike ways.

Train your children to pause, to wait, and then to wait some more. Delay the immediate reaction to fight or flee. The angry child may need to remove himself temporarily, "I need a few minutes to think about how I'm going to respond to this." Help him out by saying, "I can see you are angry. Do you need to remove yourself so you can think about a helpful way to respond?" Scripture talks about responding slowly rather than reacting quickly. "My dear brothers and sisters, take note of this: Everyone should be quick to listen, slow to speak and slow to become angry" (James 1:19).

Encourage your kiddos to develop what I call a rage interrupter. Find a go-to reaction to implement that will refocus the mad. This moves the child out of the emotional and reactive limbic system to the prefrontal cortex where reasoning occurs. I close my eyes and do a silent scream in my head. This vision helps me find a little humor in the situation. Then I'm ready to reason rather than rage. James reminds us how our words can make us look like a hypocrite if we are unable to speak with temperance. "Those who consider themselves religious and yet do not keep a tight rein on their tongues deceive themselves, and their religion is worthless" (James 1:26).

Teach your child to define the emotion. When we can pinpoint our anger to its primary emotion (embarrassment, frustration, irritation) our brain is ready to deal with the problem at hand. In essence we are catching the thought and feeling while placing it in its proper box, "We take captive every thought to make it obedient to Christ" (2 Corinthians 10:5).

Once an outburst is avoided and the feeling named, the problem that triggered the anger needs to be addressed. When our kids become skilled at conflict resolution they are no longer threatened by a little adversity. These three steps help the individuals in conflict get to the solution side of the problem:

> State what occurred, and use facts. "You took my bike without asking."
> State the concern. "I want you to ask before you borrow my bike."
> State the emotion created. "I feel disrespected and taken advantage of when I am not asked."

These three steps identify and acknowledge the problem without using assumption or accusation. The angered person is able to honestly articulate his or her feelings. This approach moves the issue to a place that isn't personal with the expectation that it can be resolved.

The next portion of the conflict resolution process is restoration. If you are the offender, restore the relationship by asking, "How can I make it better?" (Note: none of this applies to abusive situations. Get professional help if you are in an abusive situation.) On the flip side, when apologized to, accept the apology without rehashing the conflict. I admit, this can be difficult. At least it is for me. I confess it can take me some time to move to accept the apology and drop my need to state one more point. Thankfully Tom is able to move more quickly to restoration and resolution. He helps us get to the solution side of the issue.

This process may need some guidance or coaching. We want to avoid the role of director and protector. When we insert ourselves into the conflict, we become a barrier between the two people disagreeing. Kids need to be able to directly address each other without having mom or dad run interference. Parental support, encouragement, and instruction are what our kids need to learn the skills of respectful discourse.

Train your child to think of an alternative response to an angry display. Don't remind the child how he or she reacted poorly the last time but give them time to think about and practice how to respond better the next time. Teach your child to retrain his or her brain to deal with frustrations using the new response rather than reinforce and rehearse the frustrated reaction in their mind.

Help your child to change self-talk. Rather than say, "I have a hot temper," empower and train your child to say, "I am able to choose patience and kindness. I can demonstrate control."

> *The mind governed by the flesh is death, but the mind governed by the Spirit is life and peace. The mind governed by the flesh is hostile to God; it does not submit to God's law, nor can it do so.*
> *—Romans 8:6–7*

EASILY OFFENDED

"She looks like she's from another world." The statement still resounds in my memory twenty-five years later. As you can see, I'm totally over it.

My four kids and I were seated at the Dunkin Donut counter following one of my kid's well-checks. A sweet treat was the best medicine following a painful shot. The rude observation came from the male customer seated on the stool next to me. By this time, I had become accustomed to the bizarre things people say, "Your kids all look like they have different dads," a fellow mom once observed as I dropped my little ones off at preschool.

Some people say really dumb things. My oldest child has jet-black hair and the younger ones have blond. I guess that gave people license to comment on my children's looks. To both comments I said, "Hmmm." I did not feel compelled to explain that we adopted our oldest. There was no need to engage further. (Later in the day clever comebacks flooded my brain. I wonder if God made me a little slow on the draw so I would be unable to wield the cutting words in the moment.)

Today there is a term for comments that are insensitive but where no malice was intended: microaggression. Wikipedia defines microaggression as "the casual degradation of any marginalized group" and as "generally happening below the level of awareness of well-intentioned members of the dominant culture."

Microaggression is identified by the receiver's feelings. If the person was hurt, even if the comment was not intended to harm, that is considered microaggression. In some cases folks who are accused of microaggression in the workplace are being reeducated and required to attend sensitivity training.

I believe we should raise our kids to be kind to all. We are all important and worthy in God's sight. We ought to train our kids to have empathy for another. God uses this empathy so we can support others.

We have all put our foot in our mouth at least once. I have been on the giving and receiving end of microaggression. Most of us have been on both sides of the sensitivity/insensitivity coin.

When we are the receiver of the careless or clueless messages, we have an opportunity to show grace. This could be the time to educate those who mean no harm. Perhaps microaggressive comments are moments to ask: "What do you mean?" or say, "I know you didn't mean to harm, so I'm going to show you a more sensitive way to express your words." If the heart of the person is in the right place, he or she will not mind and may appreciate a little on-the-spot education.

At the same time, we don't need to be easily offended. We can deal with issues as they arise or choose to overlook the remarks. We can embrace the "That's OK" mentality and not freak out but respond in a way that honors God.

My reaction to the aforementioned examples wasn't the best. I didn't engage well. Yet I didn't overlook the remark either. I have harbored resentful feelings. Why would I give someone that power over me?

As our kids grow, kindness and empathy need to be taught and lived so they can learn how to demonstrate love to others. When our kids gain the understanding that sometimes people are uninformed or not versed in preferred verbiage, they will be able to respond with grace.

As a society, we have become overly sensitive and easily offended. When we have a big emotional reaction to another's carelessly delivered message we are focused on ourselves not on God. Why not give people the benefit of the doubt? Why jump to offense? No one likes an insensitive bloke. However, it is also tough to converse with an overly sensitive individual.

We can put these things into perspective and learn how to deal with those who are not always so pleasant and may be a bit socially awkward. Let's train our kids (and ourselves) how to love those who are insensitive and how to respond to unkind yet unintended comments with grace. The wise message from Proverbs 19:11 reinforces this thought. "A person's wisdom yields patience; it is to one's glory to overlook an offense."

BLINDSIDED

It is one thing to deal with microaggression from a stranger; it is quite another to address the unexpected actions of a family member.

"We never saw it coming . . ."

Two moms expressed this very sentiment to me just weeks apart. Each one's world has been rocked by her young adult. In a minute, life went from pretty normal and noneventful to nightmarish. Both had a daughter dabbling in behavior they never expected.

So what is a parent to do when life takes an unexpected turn? Keep living, keep loving, and keep praying. Allow the Lord to use you in drawing your child to Him. Respect the young person's right to believe or live differently from you, expect the same consideration in return, and, depending on the age and situation, establish appropriate boundaries.

We can still achieve the desired goal of interdependence within a relationship that doesn't line up philosophically. Boundaries are the way that can happen.

If our interdependent relationship is built on mutual love and respect, we do not have to do anything that violates or is in conflict with our conscience. Ultimately we will need to stand before the Lord and give an account of how we managed the life He gave us.

Sin loves company. It desires to be justified, excused, rationalized, condoned, and even validated. Comments like:

"Everyone does it."

"It's my life. No one is getting hurt. What's the big deal?"

"No one else has an issue with it. It's even legal. Why are you against this?"

Parents do not have to be unwilling participants. Do not be cajoled into partaking in any activity or pressured into stating something that makes you uncomfortable or violates your conscience, convictions, or belief system—even if it is legal.

Loving our kids in the hard places stretches us. Think of a rubber band around your wrist. Wrap it too tight, and you'll cut off your blood flow. Let it dangle loosely, and it falls off. So you must find the sweet spot, the place where the rubber band holds on but doesn't break.

Respect is a key component when it comes to establishing limits. It goes both ways. "I treat you with respect, I expect respect in return." Bridging the gap with respect and humility created by differing beliefs is worth the fight. If we want our children to be interdependent they must learn how to be respectful and proactive regarding conflict.

In Micah 6:8 it says, "He has shown you, O mortal, what is good. And what does the LORD require of you? To act justly and to love mercy and to walk humbly with your God."

We can do the right thing while displaying mercy and being humble. Parents in interdependent relationships with their older children still have influence. In Matthew 7:1–5, Jesus tells us how to deal with difficult situations.

> *Do not judge, or you too will be judged. For in the same way you judge others, you will be judged, and with the measure you use, it will be measured to you. Why do you look at the speck of sawdust in your brother's*

eye and pay no attention to the plank in your own eye? How can you say to your brother, "Let me take the speck out of your eye," when all the time there is a plank in your own eye? You hypocrite, first take the plank out of your own eye, and then you will see clearly to remove the speck from your brother's eye.

Jesus tells us not to address our brother's sin without taking care of and making note of our own. We can discuss and correct if we speak truth with a humble heart. By doing things the Matthew 7 way we will be able to maintain an interdependent relationship.

MERCY ME

We will have a home that is filled with mercy and grace if it's OK to spill and to make mistakes. Without understanding what it means to be wrong and wronged, forgive and be forgiven, we can never fully grasp grace. Conflict in relationship is an opportunity to learn mercy and grace.

New dad and counselor Kegan Mosier says this about mercy as it relates to parenting:

> Everyone said that having children would completely change our lives. I now know this to be true. No one has thrown out an, "I told you so," but if they did, I would humbly receive it. My wife and I went on a date this week and reflected on times gone by where we would take a day trip to the mountains to snowshoe for hours on end, spend a whole weekend skiing on the slopes, or take an entire Saturday to explore our city.
>
> Things are different now. Although we still go to the mountains and explore Denver, adjustments have to be made for our baby, which can quickly change predetermined expectations and lead to frustration.

Most parents, if they are honest, would agree that when the whining, temper-tantrums, screaming, and teething pains come, accessing mercy and patience can feel like grasping at straws. Momentarily, we internally lose it. Guilt attempts to make its assault on our mind. A warm wash of shame tries to cover us and convince us we are bad parents.

Parenting is a huge responsibility, accompanied with a sense of power that must be properly stewarded. I can only wield that kind of power with a heart drenched in humility. As parents, we are called to represent His character, His mercy, to our children.

Grace, mercy, and forgiveness are intertwined. Forgiveness pardons the offense. Mercy is not getting what is deserved for our actions or attitudes. Grace gives us what we don't deserve in light of the offense. Jesus is our perfect example of these qualities.

> *Humility is the fear of the LORD; its wages are riches and honor and life. —Proverbs 22:4*

CHAPTER 5

DRAWN TOGETHER WITH PEOPLE SMARTS

Live in harmony with one another. Do not be proud,
but be willing to associate with people of low position.
Do not be conceited. —Romans 12:16

"Mom, do you want to meet me in the Philippines when my contract is up?"

My twenty-four-year-old daughter Samantha wanted to know if I would meet her, vacation with her, and travel with her for ten days in Asia when her Taiwanese teaching contract expired.

My joy exploded with a big, "Yes!"

We had a great time exploring and hanging out. This was the first time ever I had that much concentrated alone time with any of my kiddos with the exception of my first child, prior to the second arriving on the scene.

On the eleventh day I was back in Colorado. Jet lag due to the fourteen-hour time difference took its toll. But as parents all know, when you return from a vacation, you hit the ground running.

The following day, I drove almost an hour-and-a-half from my home in Morrison to Colorado Springs to attend a conference. While sitting in a discussion group of twelve, I did the sleepy head bob. At the conclusion of the two-day event, I grabbed my empty water bottle and strolled over to the rectangular table draped with a white tablecloth. Round silver plates were filled with chocolate chips cookies. Next to the sweet treats was a clear container with a silver spigot that held the water. Floating in the receptacle were orange and cucumber slices. I wanted to bathe in this refreshing looking water.

A sharply dressed woman with beautifully manicured nails and carefully applied makeup moved into my bubble. I wondered if she thought I was taking too long to fill my thermos. I gave her a reassuring smile to let her know I noticed her, and I was almost done. Apparently, my demeanor gave her permission to address me.

"Oh, honey," her voice was bathed in a sweet southern drawl—you know, the only American accent that allows the speaker to say just about anything. "Don't you just wish you could take those cucumbers out and put them on the bags under your eyes?"

Bless her heart, my smile shortened and my puffy eyes crinkled. I took a giant step backward. Unkindness separates and disconnects.

BE A FRIEND

Kindness connects. It reaches out and naturally brings people together.

"How was your day?" I recall a time in high school when I asked my friend that simple question. Tami thanked me for inquiring. At that moment I realized I didn't typically ask. I reasoned if there was something noteworthy, she would just tell me. But by not asking I sent the unintended message I was not interested in her day-to-day life. Of course I was, but my actions sent a different message. Her comment let me know she wanted me to enter that space with her. Her small encouragement made a big difference in my approach to her and to my other friends.

Family members and peers train us in the art of interaction. Some kids don't know how to make friends or they need help being a friend. Some may be socially awkward; others may be emotionally or socially delayed. Our kids need our help to navigate peer relationships and maintain friendships.

"Teens today need training in everyday courtesies. I have to actually train my teen employees to greet people who walk into the shop, and I need to teach them to look customers in the eye while talking." This comment came from a business owner. She is not alone in her evaluation of teen workers. Since she mentioned her frustration, I have heard others in similar positions express the same sentiment.

Historically, people have simply caught on to how to best interact with others. Subtle interactions and nonverbal communication were observed and then imitated. Apparently what used to be noticed and practiced is now slipping past many young people. Perhaps we are too distracted with devices and schedules to lift our heads, see life around us, and interact with others.

Dr. Kathy Koch, author of *Screens and Teens: Connecting with Our Kids in a Wireless World*, says this, "Children don't value conversations and face-to-face interactions as much as children from past generations. Technology has interfered with their ability to do face-to-face communication well." She lists some ways moms, dads, and grandparents can train kids to be better communicators: slow down and enunciate, appropriately use and interpret body language and facial expressions, listen and ask questions, avoid gossip, tell the truth, don't exaggerate, answer questions by giving enough but not too much information, and demonstrate humility when our observations or assumptions are incorrect. Training our kids how to communicate well will help them create solid friendships.

PHONY BALONEY

Demonstrating an interest in people doesn't mean being fake. Looking back, I recall how my youth pastor attempted to connect with his students by using hip lingo. We thought his efforts were ridiculous. In our tween eyes, we saw an ancient thirty-year-old dad trying to fit in with a group of students by using words he perceived to be cool. In conversation, he would randomly toss in 70s slang words and phrases like "right on," "far out," and "can you dig it." *Groovy* even popped out of his mouth, but that was *so* 60s.

None of us dug it. We saw through his attempts to be someone he wasn't. We didn't talk like that anyway.

Parents, we don't have to change our language or our looks in order to fit in. Being true to who we are communicates sincerity. Trying to be someone we are not leaves people thinking we are imposters.

The bridge begins by finding the common ground of agreement upon which to build. A very tattooed and pierced receptionist, easily twenty-five years younger than I was, checked me into my MRI appointment. I had hurt my back three months earlier while waterskiing and decided it was time to figure out what was wrong. The young receptionist had ink or a hole on every inch of his exposed skin.

I have a few piercings of my own. To prepare for my MRI, I needed to remove all my jewelry. When I removed the earring from my upper ear, a cartilage piercing, the little ball from the hoop dropped to the floor and rolled under the baseboard. I was unable to retrieve it.

As I was handing my paperwork to the receptionist, I asked, "Where's the closest tattoo parlor?" He seemed surprised and a bit uncertain as to why I was asking this question.

"I lost the little ball part of my earring when I removed it for the procedure."

He brightened. We chatted for a number of minutes about what type of earring I needed, where I ought to go, and what places had specials going on. He gave me some additional information, "Did you know you can get good deals on tattoos around Halloween?" I told him I'd keep that in mind.

We found a common interest despite our age difference and appearance. That conversation was a highlight of my day. It appeared it was a high point for him too. Connection feels good.

WISE WAYS

Mary is the wisest person I know. She innately understands people and is able to articulate feelings and meaning with great accuracy. Not only is she people-smart brilliant, she also has a calming presence. When it comes to her emotional intelligence (EI), she ranks at the top of the class.

My admiration for Mary is great. I want to be like her. Here's the good news. I can up my EI game, maybe not to Mary level, but I can improve. The emotional intelligence, or emotional quotient, is a skill that can be nurtured and grown in ourselves and in our children, and it consists of four parts:

Self-Awareness: The ability to recognize and name emotions and how they affect thoughts and actions and to know emotional triggers and have a true assessment of personal strengths and weaknesses. Help your kids recognize triggers, name their emotions, and identify strengths and weaknesses: "I see by the way you are holding your head in your hands you feel frustrated. Math is a frustrating subject for you."

Self-Regulation: The will to operate out of the head rather than emotions, to control impulsive behavior, and to be reliable, flexible, and take initiative. "You feel angry. When you are ready to solve this problem you will need to work out of the thinking part of your mind. Let me know when you are ready to allow your brain to be in charge so we can get to the solution side of this struggle."

Other-Person Awareness: The ability to utilize skills of interest and empathy to put the focus on the other person by asking noninvasive general questions and listening. Empathy is best taught by experience; however, it can be learned. Any struggle is an opportunity to learn compassion. Train your kids to pick up on nonverbal social cues. Use a mirror to help identify what feelings look like. If your child is socially immature, train him to give people personal space by imagining a bubble around each person. Teach your child to be a team player and how to share credit when experiencing success.

Friendship Focus: The ability to put forth the appropriate effort in maintaining friendships and spending and making time for friends (without monopolizing, taking advantage, or controlling the other person). Train your kids to be respectful so they are able to disagree without being disagreeable, to win or lose with grace, and resolve conflict without using personal attacks.

For our kids to be a friend and have friends they must be able to show empathy, focus on others, respond to stress without blaming others, take responsibility for their actions, give grace, think before acting, and be aware of how their actions and feelings affect those around them. When our kids are able to value another person, listen, show interest, and demonstrate compassion, they will be on the right track to being a good friend.

We are naturally drawn to those who care about us and are genuine, positive, and good listeners. We avoid those who are self-absorbed, needy, or highly pessimistic. Individuals who possess high emotional intelligence tend to have good, solid friendships and easily make friends. With training and practice we can increase our own and our child's emotional intelligence.

EI ON STEROIDS

Strengths exaggerated become weaknesses. Those who have highly developed emotional intelligence are sensitive and tuned into others. They may be more likely to fall into the people pleaser category. Often the more compliant and conflict avoidant the child, the more likely he or she will be a people pleaser.

Dale Wilsher, life coach and blogger, says this in her blog post, "People Pleasing Is Not God Pleasing":

> People pleasing is a tendency some children demon-strate that causes them to focus on the approval of others. Every child wants to be loved and accepted, and many kids learn that in order to receive that love they need to earn it by "being" or "doing" what others like. People pleasing, which starts as parent pleasing, originates as children are loved conditionally when

conforming to the needs and desires of their families. Instead of becoming more of the unique person God intended them to be, people-pleasing children become social chameleons, changing their personalities, thoughts, and emotions to match their environment so they can meet their very real needs for love, acceptance, and security. What is important to note is that people pleasing is not pleasing to God. It's not a loving pattern or a good problem to have; it's selfish tactic, a way to meet our own needs because we are focused on our own image—being liked, avoiding conflict, and looking good—not on loving and serving others.

I know a young man who changes personalities like the rest of us change clothes. Depending on who is in the room determines the mask he wears. I believe this comes from his need to be accepted and to belong. He may have developed this quality as a coping mechanism due to fear or anxiety over making and keeping friends. I'm not certain he even knows who he is. I wish this young man knew he didn't need to do this. His uniqueness makes him special and delightful to be around.

Laura Petherbridge, coauthor of *The Smart Stepmom*, offers these questions in her blog post, "Why Can't I Say No?" for 1corinthians13parenting.com to use to self-evaluate our people-pleasing tendencies:

Do you . . .
Avoid conflict at all costs?
Feel guilty saying no?
Have a sense of dread, fear, or anger if not in control of a situation?
Hear yourself saying, "It's not really that bad," or, "I'm the reason this happens"?
Fear retaliation or removal of love if you say no?

Walk on eggshells, even in your own home?

Think submission means ignoring or tolerating destructive behavior?

Allow people to speak to you in a disrespectful manner?

Make excuses for rude and offensive behavior of others?

Isolate or fear what people think of you?

Refuse to discuss problems or seek help?

Take on the responsibility for someone who is irresponsible or negligent?

Try to control others with a feeling of superiority or treat your spouse like a child?

Distort God's teaching about love and mercy into ignoring sin?

I give an affirmative response to a couple of Laura's questions. I am a people pleaser. Laura's first question I answer with a resounding *yes*. I attempt to avoid conflict at all costs. I am highly sensitive to other people's emotions and do my best to avoid upsetting someone else. Tom prefers to have me stay home when he goes car shopping. The price negotiations make me uncomfortable, and I end up feeling badly for the salesman. My attempts to smooth things over with compromise are not appreciated by my thrifty deal-making husband. I like people to like me. I don't like to disappoint others. I say yes when I should say no. Some of my tendencies have rubbed off on my four kids. I don't want them to believe love is conditional or that they are responsible for another person's happiness. Plus I want my young adults to be able to swing a good deal on a car. I advise them, "Take Dad, he's your let's-make-a-deal guy. It is best to leave me out of it."

UNHEALTHY HELPING

On the surface, enabling can look like interdependence, but it is actually codependence . Enabling presents itself as a helpful action, but it is really self-serving. People pleasing or enabling meets the enablers' need to be liked, needed, or accepted. It is doing a favor with strings attached.

Melinda Means, author and life coach, considers herself a recovering people pleaser. In her blog post, "Are you a people-pleasing parent?" on her *New Thing Creations* blog, she says, "I hate conflict. For years, I considered this a virtue. . . . I was the peacemaker. [I] rarely rocked the boat. . . . Good Christian girls don't make waves. Making other people happy was the right thing to do.

"I thought I was noble. And then I had children. . . . My noble people-pleasing tendencies had hit a crossroads. The only way I could avoid conflict and make my kids happy was to give in to them. However, the more I tried to appease them, the more unhappy and demanding they seemed to become. . . .

"I gave way too many second chances. 'No' didn't really mean 'no.' It was the starting point of negotiations with Mom. I required far too little responsibility of them because it would often cause full-blown drama. The quest for all this 'happiness' came into ironic full bloom in the middle school years. All those yeses that should have been no's resulted in a lack of respect. The responsibility that wasn't given gave way to an air of entitlement. . . .

"I had to make a crushing acknowledgement: I wanted my children to be happy. However, my overriding desire was for *my own* happiness. That was the root of my people pleasing. Their approval, their happiness, was really about filling a void within myself. A void only God could fill. . . .

"God slowly showed me how to quit looking to my kids for my worth. It has been a long, painful—and incredibly freeing—process.

"The road to a healthy, respect-filled relationship with my kids hasn't progressed in a straight line. Sometimes I fall back into old patterns. . . . When I'm unsure about whether to say yes to one of my kids' request, I've found it helpful to ask myself a few questions:

"Is this about my comfort?

"Will saying yes to this bring my kids closer to being an adult who is responsible, giving, and loving?

"Is this an area where I can give grace or do I need to stand firm?

"Setting new boundaries—and enduring the resulting pushback—has been hard for me and my kids. But we are all better for it."

Children are dethroned when parents change their people pleasing tactics from "OK, whatever you want, just so you are happy" to a God-honoring agenda, "I want God's best for you." Then God reclaims His rightful place in the family, and choices and decisions made are God honoring rather than people pleasing. Most kids will respond like Melinda's and attempt to regain their king-of-the-hill status. The change may be painful for both the child and the parent, but as Melinda confirms, you and your kids are better for it.

> *We are not trying to please people but God, who tests our hearts.* —1 Thessalonians 2:4

RIGHTS ARE RIGHT

Needs and wants, rights and privileges tend to get confused. "I *need* a cell phone." "I'm sixteen, it's *my right* to drive."

Here are five rights your kids can, and ought to, embrace. These rights spill over into all relationships. If your children know these rights and rehearse them in the family, they will be empowered to apply these concepts to other significant relationships and situations.

The right to be treated with respect.
- Teach your child to ask, "Am I being treated with respect?"
- Train your child to say, "I treat you with respect, I expect respect in return."
- Show your child that because he or she (and his or her fellow humans) is created in God's image, all people are worthy of respect.
- Instruct your child in God's Word: So God created mankind in his own image, in the image of God he created them; male and female He created them. —Genesis 1:27

The right to respectfully express feelings, opinions, and expectations.

- Teach your child to say, "I feel, " "I think, " and "I'd like. "
- Train your child to avoid blaming, shaming, or using personal attacks: "You make me feel," "Your opinion is dumb," or "You should have. "
- Show your child it is OK to change their mind. It takes maturity to reconsider and readjust when assumptions have been made or opinions have been formed without all the facts.
- Instruct you child in God's Word: The way of fools seems right to them, but the wise listen to advice. —Proverbs 12:15

The right to agreeably disagree while discussing differences.

- Teach your child to listen and consider another's point of view.
- Train your child how to back up his opinions and beliefs with facts rather than emotion.
- Show your child how to respectfully disengage when discussions get heated.
- Instruct your child in God's Word: Fools find no pleasure in understanding but delight in airing their own opinions. —Proverbs 18:2

The right to discuss whether expectations and demands from another are reasonable.

- Teach your child to ask, "Is this expectation reasonable?"
- Train your child to inquire, "Do I have a say in this?"
- Show your child healthy relationships are reciprocal, not one-sided.
- Instruct your child in God's Word: Wisdom will save you from the ways of wicked men. —Proverbs 2:12

The right to wait and ponder before giving an answer.

- Teach your child to wait in order to think things through before deciding.

- Train your child to say, "I will think about this and get back to you later."
- Show your child how to evaluate the pros and cons when making a decision.
- Instruct your child in God's Word: Let the wise listen and add to their learning, and let the discerning get guidance. —Proverbs 1:5

By understanding these rights, our child is less likely to be vulnerable to peer pressure, a victim of bullying, a people pleaser, influenced by a sales pitch or scam, or in a controlling or abusive relationship.

We can equip our children to recognize manipulation and persuasion. They will be empowered by learning these five fundamental rights. We can encourage and prepare them by putting these five principles into practice in our family.

When we are able to understand and respond to other's emotions and behaviors while maintaining our personal rights, we can have healthy interdependent and well-connected relationships. Families with these characteristics won't disintegrate or fall apart when somebody spills. As parents we are in the position to help our kids increase and strengthen their emotional intelligence. We can show them how to draw people in by demonstrating interest, train them to avoid people-pleasing behaviors, and to recognize manipulation. We want our kids to have kind, healthy, and interdependent relationships not dependent or codependent friendships.

> I led them with cords of human kindness, with ties of love. To them I was like one who lifts a little child to the cheek, and I bent down to feed them. —Hosea 11:4

CHAPTER 6

SIMPLE EVERYDAY CONNECTIONS

But encourage one another daily, as long as it is called "Today," so that none of you may be hardened by sin's deceitfulness. —Hebrews 3:13

Murphy, my sixty-pound, rust-colored labradoodle, is all about being with his people. He has two favorite things—cuddling and going for a w-a-l-k. Eating takes third place. Murphy is a social eater. His breakfast bowl remains untouched until his humans are around. He has even been known to fill his mouth with kibble, take a few steps from the kitchen to the family room, and drop it on the carpet before consumption so he remains in the center of our family activity.

My big red dog reminds me life is about being together. I can get swept up in being the keeper of lists, the manager of stuff, and the administrator of the daily schedule to the point that I forget to connect. My words are more instructional or functional than relational. I define success by efficiently working my list, effectively running the household, and keeping the schedule—good for a worker, not so good for a mother or a wife.

As a parent and spouse, I want connection with my family to be my measure of success. It isn't easy to do this, especially if you have a task-orientated personality. I often look at interruptions and schedule changes as an inconvenience rather than an opportunity to connect. Setting aside my plan for the day and being open to what God has or what one of my family members may need isn't easy. When my kids were little I got lots of practice with being flexible. But even after all the training from my children I am still not skilled in this area. I wonder, "Is my issue more selfishness than rigidity?" If I truly mean business, I will seek to intentionally connect each day through conversation, action, affection, and acknowledgement. And I will be willing to release my tight grip on my agenda.

TIME SPENT

Time spent together, scheduled or impromptu, is one of the best ways to build relationships and demonstrate love. Prior to an event at a local church where I was scheduled to speak, I had the pastor approach their fifth and sixth grade students and have them fill out a card, "What I wish my parents knew about me." I shared the answers with the moms and dads the following weekend at the workshop. The top answer was, "I wish they knew I want them to spend more time with me." The parents were surprised. They were expecting, "I need a cell phone," or, "I need more privacy."

Jenna Hallock, mom and executive director of Family Time Training, nails it: "Time is the currency of relationship, and the more you spend, the stronger your relationship." Time spent together strengthens the family bonds.

Jenna asked her son Eli and daughter Zoe to help her come up with some everyday, easily implemented ideas on things a parent and child can do together.

"Basketball is my favorite. I love shooting hoops with my dad!" Eli, ten, is a sports enthusiast. Jenna expands, "If [your child is] passionate about a sport . . . take the time to learn the skills and rules if you don't already know them, and encourage him to practice side-by-side and to work hard to do his best for God's glory."

Eli adds, "On our trip to Yellowstone, mom and I hiked to the top of Paint Pot. The view was awesome. We took pictures and videos on the way. It was one of my favorite parts."

Jenna emphasizes adventure is a great way to bond. "[Kids] are natural adventure seekers. Whether it's trying a new restaurant, flying a kite, fishing, or going on a nature walk, you can cultivate and support that spirit of adventure by making plans to do these things together."

Jenna's family also likes to play Chopped where they make dishes using odd ingredients. Eating and cooking together teaches the kids how to make family favorites and try out new recipes. Cooking confidence is gained by working together in the kitchen and then savoring the fruits of your labor.

Jenna's daughter, thirteen-year-old Zoe includes, "Dress up!" Jenna agrees, "This is one of the most fun things for a mom and daughter to do together. Whether it's getting out the princess dresses and comically sized pearls, or going to your daughter's favorite store and letting her try on things to her heart's desire, it is a good way to make her feel special, have fun together, and remind her that she is beautiful in God's eyes and yours."

I asked some other moms from the Moms Together Facebook group (supportive and encouraging group of moms and grandmoms) what they do to connect with their kids. Here are their clever and easily implemented ideas:

> I have nighttime chats with my nineteen-year-old. Sometimes, she'll even text me during the day to tell me she has something she can't wait to tell me about at our nightly chat. She stores things up throughout the day for it. —Elizabeth Spencer, mom of two

> I have two very different daughters; connecting looks different with each. With my fourteen-year-old, staying up late Friday nights to watch a movie, just the two of us, is treasured time she enjoys. Outings to the library or bookstore are meaningful to her because of her love for books. Then we top off the day with ice cream or anything chocolate. My younger daughter, age twelve, loves to shop. We venture to retail outlets and do crafts together or play board games. We all love walking our Labrador retriever together. In fact, ever since we got a dog, we have had

way more opportunities to connect. It forces us out of the house away from distractions that sadly can prevent us from focusing on one another, as crazy as that sounds! —Linda Tang, mom of two

We go apple or berry picking. Apple picking requires teamwork; working together is something that needs to be practiced at all ages. —Janice Powell, mom of three

We create an art gallery. Everyone draws a few pictures with crayons and markers. Then we hang our creations on the curtains. The "artist" tours us through the gallery and explains the drawings. At the conclusion of the tour, the gallery curator (Mom), hands out champagne glasses of juice and everyone gathers for cookies. —Lisa Leshaw, mom of two, grandma of six

Family trivia is our game. The group is given multiple-choice questions about the family. The other players have to guess the answer. It's usually pretty fun. This is one way my husband and I teach our kids about our family history. This game spurs on conversations about hopes, dreams, and some deeper things. —Michelle Nietert, therapist and mom of two

My three kids start school an hour apart. I'm able to snuggle in bed with each of them for twenty minutes. This sets a great tone for the day. —Jamie Bates, mom of three

My family enjoys highly interactive games like Would You Rather, hiking, or going on walks while taking photos of each other. I have discovered this shows how the photographer views family members and the world. —Rachel Robins, mom of five

Every night, we have a special time with our four-year-old son just before we tuck him in that we call "favorite things." We share our favorite parts of the day, which helps us look for joy on even the worst or most mundane days. Then we ask, "What are you proud of today?" That helps him think about what he did well, regardless of adult judgment. We then tell him what we saw him doing well during the day. It's a lovely, quiet time of reflection for all of us to wind down at the end of the day. —Shannon Brescher Shea, mom of two

Twenty Extra Minutes is a strategy we use. We got this idea from YourModernFamily.com. On the day of your kid's birthday of each month, allow that child to stay up twenty minutes later than their siblings for some one-on-one time with parents. (For example, if your child's birthday is July 11, he or she can stay up twenty minutes later with mom and dad on the eleventh of every month.) —Kristi Drullard Kohn, mom of three

Not to be left out, dads have great ideas on ways to connect. These ideas may not always carry "The Mom Seal of Approval." In fact, try these ideas at your own risk. They tend to be more physical, messy, and include a little risk. Kids love dad ideas! Mom, it's important to move out of the way and let dad create his own connections.

I love wrestling with my kids. They love it too. We also like to play marshmallow wars. We each get a handful of marshmallows and throw them at each other. It is like an indoor snowball fight. —Nate Havens, dad of two

My girls love to play hide-and-go-seek in the dark. When they find me I chase after them while doing some scary screaming. They love this game! —Jayson Graves, dad of two

The kids climb into the laundry basket, and I let them slide down the stairs—although we did put a hole in the wall once, and another time the basket tipped and the kids fell out. I also let my kids finger paint in their underwear. A little milder, less messy and dangerous game we like to play we call hot and cold. I hide one of their stuffed animals and say hot or cold to help the kids find the toy. The closer they are to the hidden toy the hotter they get while cold indicates moving further from discovery. —Ed Millard, dad of four

When my kids were little, I'd put plastic sea creatures in the bathtub and let them play Sea World. I would be the announcer, and the kids would manipulate the dolphins and killer whales as if they were doing tricks in the water. The floor would get soaked. They had so much fun splashing and making a mess! —Tom, dad of four

The investment of time will make memories for a lifetime and strengthen the family relationships. With our young adult kids we love to play family games. Cribbage, Catch Phrase, and card games rank among the favorites. The competition is friendly and lively. To celebrate our thirty-fifth anniversary, Tom and I rented a house in the Cayman Islands. It was a once-in-a-lifetime type of vacation. We invited the entire Wildenberg crew. The three unmarried kids were able to bring a guest. All parties were responsible for their own plane ticket and every pair made two dinners. Tom and I took care of the breakfasts, lunches, and snacks. Everyone had to bring a game or two to share. Each evening we watched the sunset and played games. During the day we relaxed, read, snorkeled, and kayaked. Distributing the responsibility for food and entertainment was part of the fun. These moments, the small impromptu times and the bigger scheduled trips, open up space for laughter and conversation. Time together prepares both littles and young adults to be more willing to invest in family relationships and discuss important life topics. (See the appendix for more ideas for daily connections with kids and grandkids of any age, page 175.)

TABLE TALK

Dinner is a great time to come together. Having the family dinner be a priority is a commitment. There were many times my kids traded the kitchen chair for the backseat of the car. Kids were fed on the move and in between activities.

As often as the six of us were able to eat together, we'd gather around the table, and Tom and I would say, "Tell us about your day." Typically our eldest would go first and expand on her day, the middle two would give an abbreviated version of the last ten hours, and the youngest would begin by saying, "Well, I woke up. Then . . ." By the time five-year-old Kendra concluded, the other three kids were slumped in their chairs with their eyes glazed over. Due to their differing personality styles, Tom and I learned we needed to draw out the middle two with more specific questions and help the bookends condense their experiences. We changed our statement to a question, "What was the high and what was the low part of your day?"

Research shows that family meals are important. Yet for many they can be a challenge. We do not have to have a formal gathering to connect. Connection just has to be deliberate.

Here are a few conversation starters we can use with our kiddos. These openers give us a glimpse into our children's world:

Who did you sit next to at lunch?
What did you do at recess?

Who did you play with?
What made you smile today?
How did you make someone smile today?
How did you make God smile today?
What was the highlight of your day?
What was the low point of your day?
Which two feeling words describe your mood today? Why?

The key is to ask questions that spur conversation; answers that require more than a yes, no, or fine response. To expand the conversation, additional statements and questions are helpful: "Tell me more," "How did you feel about that?" and "What would you do differently?" By doing this we can enter our kiddo's world without being intrusive. There is an added benefit of building our child's social and conversational skills.

SPEAK TEEN

Shut doors, lowered heads, texting fingers, rolling eyes, and big sighs all communicate, "Leave me alone." Yet most teens really do want to connect with their parents. Teens do have some expectations regarding connection. They want some control over the place, time, and topic. The exchange must be authentic. Before beginning a conversation, show respect for their schedule and ask, "Is now a good time to chat?" or, "When is a good time to talk?" Notice your teen's nonverbal communication. Is she too tired to talk? Has there been an unresolved rift in your relationship that needs to be repaired? If so, address this first. Does this conversation need to be confidential? If so, find a private time and place.

When talking with your teen, be careful not to fire off a series of questions. This feels intrusive. The goal is to be relational, not instructional. Avoid interrogation, criticism, coercion, and advisement. Seek understanding, reserve judgment, and listen. Encourage critical thinking skills by asking open-ended questions.

Krista Van Allen, the founder of Girl Above, a ministry to teen girls, interviewed a group of young women. She posed this question, "What do you wish your parents knew?" Here's their list: high school and societal pressure is intense, they want their parents to be honest and real, they need love and patience from their parents to get through the day, high school problems may be different from parental problems but they are big to the teen, and please don't add to the drama.

These comments give us insight into what our teens need. Understanding, calm, compassion, and empathy appear to be top of the list. Surprisingly, they want moms and dads to be more in the know. Here are some questions that will get us to a deeper level of intimacy with our kids: What sort of peer pressure do most high school students experience? (It is less intense if this question is more general than personal, say *students* rather than *you*.) What is your biggest struggle right now? Where do you feel happy and successful? What do you appreciate or admire about your friends? If you could change something about your friends, family, church, or school what would you change?

Recently Tom went out to breakfast with a young man who is dating one of our girls. Our daughter's boyfriend wanted to have time alone to talk man-to-man with Tom. The purpose was solely for the two men to get to know each other. Over coffee and pancakes, Tom was blown away by this question, "Do you have any advice for me?" It isn't often a young person seeks advice. Of course, Tom was more than happy to offer some thirty-five years of marital wisdom. "Be best friends and be able to forgive each other."

Our young adult kids prefer to ask for or to be asked before advice is dispensed or experiences are shared. Connection at this stage is the goal. Here are some tender ways to do that: Would you like some advice? Do you want help figuring this out? Would you like to hear my thoughts or experience with this? How should I pray for you?

Our young people want to connect in a real and authentic way. They need to hear about things we wrestled with, times where we got it right and times when we got it wrong. They desire transparency.

When we push pride and perfection aside we are able to be real so a heart-to-heart connection can grow.

KNOW THE STORY

Time needs to be carved out for our kids to hear our stories. Filling them in on our lives connects our hearts with theirs; we become more human to our children. We need to hear their stories as well so we can fully appreciate them. When they have some insight into our past struggles and fears, they feel safe sharing theirs. When we know our kids well we are better able to understand what motivates, scares, or angers them.

Nina, a Bible teacher, was presenting the story in Acts 15:36–41 to a classroom of teens. Paul and Barnabas agreed to part ways because of a disagreement. Paul did not want John Mark to join them on their missionary journey because he had deserted them on a previous trip. Barnabas wanted John Mark to come along. This caused the men to continue on their mission but to go separate ways.

Nina asked, "Who do you side with? Paul or Barnabas?" Most of the students felt Paul made the best decision. Then she said, "What if John Mark deserted them because he got word his daughter was dying?" That detail made a difference to the class. Now they could understand John Mark's reason for leaving.

"Sometimes a young woman may have a reputation of being promiscuous. But what if you took the time to find out her story? What if she had been molested? Would that make a difference in your view of her? I know a young man who appears to be a braggart. As it turns out he received little to no encouragement from his father. He brags to fill the hole left by a lack of support from his dad. When we go deeper and discover people's stories we are less likely to judge them on their pain."

We don't know why John Mark deserted Paul and Barnabas. Scripture doesn't tell us. The point of Nina's exercise was to have the young men and women look further into the whys rather than just see an action. Understanding the reason people talk or act like they do helps us to connect with compassion.

Sometimes our kids choose to do things that on the surface look like a poor decision. Dig a little further to gain more knowledge and understanding of the full reason for the behavior.

SMALL CONNECTIONS, BIG MEMORIES

Heart-to-heart connection is mostly developed in everyday, simple ways. We don't have to do the big events to create a memory or strengthen a relationship. Roni Wing Lambrecht is a mom who learned this truth due to a traumatic event.

"As a new mom to Dalton in 1998, I fell head first into planning momentous occasions for my family, from over-the-top birthday parties to cruises, Walt Disney World, and more.

"I vividly remember the week before our big camping trip to Glamis Sand Dunes in 2013. Fifteen-year-old Dalton was exhausted from his high school finals. He asked, 'Can we just chill for a few minutes?' I quickly responded with, 'No, babe, we'll have plenty of time for that next week. We have so much work to do before we go that we just don't have time to slow down right now. I promise it will all be worth it when we get there.'

"We headed for Glamis just a few days after that conversation. Once there, we celebrated Christmas with just the three of us. We had several days to ride our ATVs. We were free to eat, sleep, and chill according to our own schedule. What a blessing. It was the perfect week—until Sunday morning at 10:37 a.m. Pacific time.

"Dalton was on his ATV riding through the dunes, enjoying every second, when he was hit head-on by a sand rail, an off-road motor vehicle. He was killed instantly. How could this be happening? What did we do to deserve this? No more Christmases or birthdays. No more trips together.

"One day, while I was feeling especially regretful, a friend asked me, 'If Dalton was standing right here and I asked him if his mom loved him, what would he say?'

"He would tell you, 'Yes, I was very loved.'

"'How would he know that?'

"I'm not sure exactly how I answered her that day, yet that was a profound question. Little things communicated great love in our family. He knew he was loved.

"We cuddled every night before bed and often in the mornings too. We made breakfast and dinner and did dishes together. We danced and sang together. We went grocery shopping, folded laundry, and cleaned the house together. We worked on homework together. He often went to work appointments with me. We loved a lot of the same musicians, television shows, books, and games. He hugged me every morning in the kitchen between the fridge and the island.

"When I look back, I am so thankful we had all those little, meaningful moments along our journey. Those memories are the ones that bring comfort and help me get through the day."

Roni reminds us to cherish those little moments with our loved ones. Those are the times that matter most.

FRAGMENTED AND FRENZIED

Pete Larson of Family Fest Ministries shares his life changing experience.

"I was building a twenty-six foot retaining wall in my front yard. A concrete saw rental was necessary. I was determined to save $35 and get the saw returned within the hourly rental time. I made my last cut, loaded the saw, and headed back to the rental store with two minutes to spare.

"While driving, I noticed a child running across the four-lane road. It seemed odd in an industrial area, and the child looked young. As I passed him I quickly glanced around looking for other children or adults.

"'Should I stop and check? I have two minutes to get the saw back.' I reasoned, 'There must be someone with him.'

"I continued on my mission to return the saw. As I returned to my car I was still thinking about that little boy. *Why didn't I stop? What if he was alone? If I hurry, maybe I can find him.*

"I drove back and saw him standing on the sidewalk. 'Thank God,' I said as I pulled over and got out of the car.

"'Hey buddy, what are you doing out here?'

"Tears spilled out of his eyes, 'I wanna go home! I want my daddy.'

"The weightiness of the moment descended on me. I was so wrapped up in my quest and my concern about saving a few dollars that I didn't stop to help a lost child!

"A female driver pulled over and called the police. After talking with the boy, we deduced he had wandered away from a birthday party at an indoor trampoline park. While she waited with the little two year old for the police, I drove to the party center where I saw several staffers and a father frantically searching the parking lot. I explained that the boy was found and was just down the road. As I pointed down the road, the police were arriving.

"For the next few days, I couldn't get that event out of my mind. *What if the boy had tried to go back and had been hit by a car? What is wrong with me that I am so busy that I couldn't stop to help a lost child? Have I filled my life with so much busyness that I no longer have any margin in my life to stop and help someone in need?*

"A few days later I was reading the parable of the Good Samaritan in Luke 10:25–37. It dawned on me—I was the priest and the Levite—a busy person with no margin to serve.

"'Forgive me, Lord. Help me with my addiction to busyness.'

"Over the past few weeks I have added to that prayer, 'God, deliver me from my need to be busy. Open my eyes to the needs around me.'"

Like Pete, I'm always on a mission. Often that mission isn't God's. Like Pete, I choose to vote no to the frenzied life. I reject the rush. I am against the fragmented family syndrome. I want perspective, eternal perspective, to dictate my day. The battle for attention and direction rages in my mind between what is good and what is best. In Luke 10:38–42, Jesus helped Martha clarify the best yes.

> *As Jesus and his disciples were on their way, he came to a village where a woman named Martha opened her home to him. She had a sister called Mary, who sat at the Lord's feet listening to what he said. But Martha was distracted by all the preparations that had*

to be made. She came to him and asked, "Lord, don't you care that my sister has left me to do the work by myself? Tell her to help me!" "Martha, Martha," the Lord answered, "you are worried and upset about many things, but few things are needed—or indeed only one. Mary has chosen what is better, and it will not be taken away from her."

From this passage Jesus teaches us time with Him is the best time. People are more important than stuff. People are more important than chores, cooking, and cleaning. And people are more important than iPhones or screen time. (OK, He doesn't say this, but I think it's implied.)

I wonder if Martha felt hurried to get things done for her guests. Pete certainly felt rushed while doing errands. I have felt hurried, pressed for time, rushed, and overwhelmed when my schedule is overloaded. My calendar is a chaotic mess. I attempt to squeeze in six individuals' crazy schedules into the little white squares. Some events bleed into the next days with an arrow to indicate the date they are supposed to occur.

One day in particular was especially crazy. Courtney needed to be picked up from marching band, Jake had to be dropped off at football practice, and Samantha and Kendra had horseback riding lessons. It was time to start dinner and for Courtney to begin her homework.

My pick up and drop off worked smoothly with Courtney and Jake. Next on my list was to get the younger girls to the stable for their lesson. Our steps quickened as we approached the barn to meet their instructor, who was late as usual. My frustration rose. The margin between drop offs and pick-ups was thin. My lips tightened, my eyes squinted, and I exhaled with emphasis. My girls observed my obvious irritation.

"Mom, go ahead and leave. We are OK. Jenny will be here any minute. We can wait here in the barn until she comes."

I mulled this over for a quick minute. I reasoned, "They are twelve and ten. They have been in this barn many times. Jenny will show up any minute."

"OK," I concurred. I would still be able to make dinner. Courtney could get going on her homework. This was making good sense. Then I'll swing by the football field and get Jake. On my return to the barn I will even have a few minutes to watch the last bit of the of the younger girls' lesson.

Courtney and I made our way home. I pulled out the pans I needed for dinner. My phone rang.

"Mom, Jenny never came. We are still here in the barn waiting." The heat rose from my feet to my head as I wondered, "How could Jenny have forgotten?"

"I'm coming back right now."

Anger was powering my resolve to go to Jenny's home on the horse property and let her know she forgot about my daughters. How dare she put my kids in this position?

I strode with purpose to her front door, with my two girls struggling to keep up with my power walking. Jenny responded to my passionate pounding and opened the front door. She had totally blown off the lesson. She was wearing sweats, not jeans. Her hair was loosely falling on her shoulders, not up in a ponytail.

"Jenny, the girls waited for you in the barn for thirty minutes."

She furrowed her brow, "Lori, their lesson is next week, not today."

My righteous indignation morphed into embarrassed remorse. "Oh, I am so sorry. We will see you in a week." I sheepishly stepped off her front porch.

"Mom . . ." both girls chimed in unison.

When I am overcommitted, highly scheduled, and have a messy calendar, life doesn't just feel out of control. It is out of control.

Becky Danielson, mom, author, and cofounder of 1 Corinthians 13 Parenting, is a planner extraordinaire. I needed her systematic approach to prevent the infamous barn incident. I've seen her calendar. She even color codes according to each family member. In her blog post, "3 Considerations to Take Control of the Family Calendar," she says, "Busy is not a badge of honor. Tame the family calendar to make family life more peaceful and calm," and adds three practical ideas on how to control the calendar chaos.

"Determine priorities. The problem isn't choosing the good activities from the bad; it's deciding what's best. Make a list of what's important to your family and use that list when making decisions about participation in various events.

"Provide limits. Children do not have to experience every sport, cultural activity, or class before they start kindergarten. The trend is to do it all and as a result is creating totally frazzled families.

"Plan a weekly family meeting to arrange the schedule. Getting the whole crew on the same page makes the family run more smoothly. . . . Taking time each week to look over the calendar . . . Begin the meeting with prayer for God's guidance. Together, examine the calendar, schedule activities, and plan family time while keeping your priorities and limits in mind."

Closely looking at our daily routine and weekly schedule is an opportunity for us to evaluate how we spend our time. When my daughter, Samantha, was in first grade she was a busy gal: gymnastics three times a week, church activities on Wednesday, and Daisies (Girl Scouts for kindergarten and first grade girls). One Saturday Tom had taken Samantha to her gymnastics practice. When he brought her home she was favoring her left arm. I ended up taking her to Urgent Care to see what was wrong. She had broken her wrist when doing a back handspring. After she got her purple cast on, she smiled from ear to ear. I thought she would be devastated that she couldn't do gymnastics for at least two months. I asked, "Why are you smiling? I thought you would feel sad." She blew me away with her response, "Well now I can spend more time with you." After that exchange, we sat down and she chose to take two practices off the table and decided not to move on from Daisies to Brownies when she became a second grader.

Lisa Brown, homeschool mom of two and parent coach, made a bold and major life change when she realized her priorities were not in sync with her desires for her family.

"I put my writing dreams on hold for another time. My husband, kids, and home were suffering because I wasn't attending to family life like I wanted to. The meals I dreamed of preparing didn't happen, our family time suffered, clutter took up living space, and my kids were not receiving the daily attention that I longed to give them.

"Writing, social media, and blogging kept me from a deeper connection with my family. After I made the decision to walk away from this, I felt my heart dance. A reservoir of creative juices inside my soul broke loose. This is who God designed me to be.

"God has filled me with creative ideas on how to connect more deeply with my family. We are proactively interacting through music, books, games, art, crafts, baking, decorating, and going on adventures. God has filled me with a creative desire to add value to the lives of the people living under my roof.

"As a result of my priority shift, my children are growing spiritually, the family is tightly bonded, and lasting memories are being made. For the first time in a very long time, I am confident what I'm doing really matters. I know I'm making a difference in my children's lives."

My Martha bent needs to move over and make room for a Mary perspective. I'm choosing to put away the time suckers and distractions in order to be present with family and friends. And whoever else the Lord may show me. Cherish loved ones by spending time together, laughing, and fully enjoying the relationships the Lord has given us. Mary teaches us about being present and listening when she sat at Jesus's feet (Luke 10:39). The Lord taught Martha what was best. Pete, Lisa, and I are learning to readjust so we can better connect with those the Lord puts in front of us. Nina's illustration causes us to see the person and seek understanding. We are powerfully reminded by Roni that it is not about the schedule. It is about the people. Interdependency draws us together through time, memories, and understanding.

But Mary treasured up all these things and pondered them in her heart. —Luke 2:19

CHAPTER 7

WATCH FOR LOOSE LINKS

As iron sharpens iron, so one person sharpens another.
—Proverbs 27:17

My afternoon was spent working on a project, and the process was frustrating. I had allotted one hour for the task, but it took me three. The type of creativity required was not a skill set I possessed, but finally all the pertinent information was applied to a semi-visually appealing layout. Time was running out and good enough had to be acceptable. I reached to switch on the printer. No response. I pressed the power button a little harder. No juice. The story of the woman speaking to the computer expert on the phone popped into my head. You know the one, where she complains her computer isn't working. The tech guru leads her through a series of checks only to discover the computer isn't plugged in. I checked the connection to the wall outlet. "Thank goodness I'm not *that* dumb." The black box continued to lay dormant. I pushed the printer to the left so I could peek at the plug attached at the back. It also appeared to be connected. In desperation I unplugged and reattached the connection. I pressed the button and voila! The white light was bright and the blue wireless icon was steady. The printer was now ready to cooperate.

The result of a loose connection can be total disconnection unless effort is exerted toward fixing it. Rivalry, grief, bitterness, blame, and resentment can all lead to a loose connection in the family. Some attitudes and certain circumstances bring on the slow fade of family relationships if we are not proactive in prevention or intervention.

ADD SIBLING CEMENT

While being dragged behind the speed boat, attempting to get up on one ski, I heard a big crack. After an MRI and a CT scan, it was discovered I hadn't pulled a muscle but rather I had broken my back.

The way to repair a vertebral compression fracture is to pour some cement into the injured area. This lessens the pain, speeds up recovery, and reduces the risk of future fractures. Fractures that are not treated will heal, but the vertebra will remain in a collapsed position. The benefit of this procedure is that the vertebra returns to a normal position before the bone hardens. My L5 vertebra is now the strongest bone in my body.

Relationship breaks happen just as accidents do. To become strong again, the rift needs some relational cement or it will forever be damaged. If care is taken to repair the damage, the relationship can be even stronger. Adversity, if addressed with wisdom and kindness, can strengthen relationships going forward.

One of the greatest heartaches a parent can experience is division between their children. Sibling rivalries are as old as time. Genesis documents the stories of Cain, Jacob, and Joseph. Cain killed his brother Abel (Genesis 4:1–8), Jacob stole his older brother Esau's birthright and blessing (Genesis 25:19—27:46), and Joseph's older brothers sold him as a slave (Genesis 37). All these relationships had the key element of jealousy.

It is easy to unknowingly sabotage the very thing we want. Comparison and competition among siblings are the catalysts for rivalry; the bigger the rivalry, the bigger the relational gap. Envy is stirred and jealousy is fostered when we compare our children to each other. Encourage and nurture each individual according to his or her unique personality and needs.

There is a video that has gone viral on You Tube titled, "Brothers of the Bride Do a Surprise Rap/Toast at Wedding Reception." It is clever, cute, and catchy. It brings joy to see positive sibling relationships. While watching the video, I realized the young adults performing were the children of my friends, Eric and Jackie Eastman.

The Eastmans's adult children get along well. They have a sense of humor, show love, and clearly enjoy each other's company—things most of us desire for our children.

I posed this question to Jackie, "What did you do to foster those strong sibling relationships?"

"It began at a very young age. My oldest son was happy when his baby brother was born. Later on both boys were thrilled to have a baby sister. I realize this isn't always the case; some kids are not as welcoming when younger siblings come along.

"We did not consciously teach the kids how to get along with one another. From the time they were little we were intentional about teaching character and having respect for others.

"My husband and I genuinely enjoy each other and we get along well. It's much easier to tell kids not to fight and argue when the parents are not fighting and arguing themselves.

"Perhaps the most important thing we did was talk. Every night at dinner one child would read the family devotional. Following the reading, we would discuss two or three questions. After that we shared the best and worst things of the day. Whenever one of the kids was hurting, the siblings would rally with encouragement and good advice. This dinner talking time knit our souls to each other and the Lord.

"Don't get me wrong; our family was not perfect. None of this came easily. There were plenty of fights and arguments. (Isn't that what kids are supposed to do?) It was up to Eric and me to teach our kids to be accountable for their actions, make apologies, and offer forgiveness. We hoped once they worked through the conflict, they would be in a better place than before.

"A respectful and fun home environment makes kids happy. Happy kids see the good in others and are more likely to get along."

There are other biblical siblings like James and John, Moses with Aaron and Miriam, and Mary with Martha and Lazarus who didn't have perfect relationships either, but they had resilient ones. The Sons of Thunder (James and John) conspired to have their mom speak to

Jesus about them sitting on either side of the Lord when He entered His kingdom (Matthew 20:20–28), Martha expressed annoyance with Mary (Luke 10:38–42), and Moses had to address Aaron's big mess with the golden calf when he returned from his forty-day meeting with God (Exodus 32).

The biblical accounts of sibling relationships reflect our own experience. Our relationships this side of heaven won't be perfect but we can do some things to make them more resilient. Differences don't have to bring disunity.

The bad actors of envy and jealousy have no place in a family that seeks interdependence. In order to keep these qualities out of the home, comparison and favoritism must not be invited in. Instead moms and dads foster relationships when we appreciate differing talents, understand unique struggles, have meaningful connections, and avoid favoritism.

Building the relationship between brothers and sisters takes parental intentionality and selflessness. As my now young adults begin their own lives and create their own living spaces, I need to remember what I value. It's important to me that my kids want to be together whether or not Tom and I are in the mix (although I have to say I love being a part of whatever they are doing).

It's easy to be in relationships that have no challenges. It's no sweat to give and receive love from people who think and believe the same way we do. My kids are each different and so are yours. They have varied interests, different walks of faith, and unique struggles and strengths. For siblings to be committed to an interdependent relationship, blood, sweat, and tears are sure to be a part of the equation. As parents we can assist in mopping up the occasional mess because we know everybody spills.

GOOD GRIEF

To move our kids to compassion they need to walk in another's shoes. Brené Brown says empathy connects while sympathy separates.

Empathy says, "I'm here with you in this hard place." Sympathy speaks, "I'm sorry you are in that hard place."

While sympathy isn't bad, it isn't great either. It leaves the individual feeling isolated and alone instead of cared for and comforted. Empathy fuels empowerment. We are able to move forward when we feel heard and understood in our struggles.

Here's what empowerment energized by experiencing empathy sounds like:

I understand sadness is a part of life.

I may grieve but I will not stay there.

I realize struggle is temporary.

I have hope.

I believe God created me for a special purpose.

I will follow God's plan for me.

Sympathy disconnects and generates blame and shame. Empathy leaves room for failure, mistakes, and grief. Empowerment spurs us on to learn, take responsibility, and have a positive outlook. We are strengthened and fortified when empathy connects us to one another and to our goals.

Jesus is our perfect example of someone who showed empathy. He became man, a great high priest, who understands our struggles (Hebrews 4:14–16). We can gain compassion when we first experience grief and sadness ourselves then apply it to circumstances other people are going through. Since we live in a fallen world, sadness is part of the package. It's up to moms and dads to teach their kids how to respond to personal sadness and other people's heartaches.

Empathy cements us together. It causes us to participate in another's healing process. It is a necessary quality for relationships in a fallen world.

THE BOUNCE

The reality of living in a fallen world is that our kids will suffer sometime in their life. None of us like this fact. Prevention and protection are natural parental actions.

Kids being raised today have been called the fragile generation. The children are protected from hardship and pain is prevented. We shield them from disappointment. We guard them from discomfort. We hover over homework to fend off failure. We are poised to pounce if they sit on the bench. We rescue, we blame, and we excuse.

We want our kids to be safe, successful, happy, and comfortable. We don't want them to struggle. Yet Jesus told the disciples in John 16:33, "In this world you will have trouble."

Suffering is part of the human experience. It produces a silver lining of perseverance, responsibility, accountability, humility, and empathy. The challenges our kids face create opportunities for emotional and spiritual growth. Creativity and problem solving abilities are birthed and confidence is cultivated. Hard times can draw our kids closer to God. Knowing this, it is easier to allow suffering to enter our kids' lives without running interference.

Give your kids a window into your own disappointments, heartaches, and failures to normalize their struggles. When suffering surfaces a parent can implement six progressive stages of response to help the child navigate difficult moments:

Experience It: Allow children to fully feel the emotions of happy and sad. Both feelings are part of the human experience. It may not feel good to be sad, but it isn't bad; it's normal. Our kids shouldn't be protected from their emotions.

Express It: Provide space for your kids to be sad. Be ready to listen and love. Share a time when you walked through a disappointing time. It's important your kids know you struggle too.

Define It: Give your kids words to frame their emotions. Mirror what you hear to help your kids name their emotions. "It sounds like you are frustrated. I'd feel frustrated too." By stating this, your children will feel heard and understood.

Deal with It: Let your kids get to the solution side of the issue. Once feelings are identified, stress is reduced and the brain is more able to deal with the problem and work toward a solution. Give your child the opportunity to be the one to come up with the way to solve a difficulty.

Learn from It: Ask questions. Help the child focus on the whats and hows, not the whys. "What is God teaching me?" "How can I respond?" Rather than, "Why me?"

Use It: God never wastes our suffering. God will at some point encourage the sufferer to reach out to and help another.

Let your kids experience suffering; express it, define it, deal with it, learn from it, and use it. If we prevent and protect our kids from hard things they will be emotionally fragile while becoming entitled and selfish. Over time they will be insecure, lack confidence, and fearful. Ultimately overprotected children will grow to resent mom and dad for their constant intervention. Instead, let's equip our kids for suffering so at some point they can help someone else.

Since we cannot prevent and protect our kids from pain, we must arm them with some spiritual truths about suffering:

It's temporary.
Though now for a little while you may have had to suffer grief in all kinds of trials. —1 Peter 1:6

God is near when we suffer.
The Lord is close to the brokenhearted and saves those who are crushed in spirit. —Psalm 34:18

And God will strengthen us.
So do not fear, for I am with you; do not be dismayed, for I am your God. I will strengthen you and help you; I will uphold you with my righteous right hand. —Isaiah 41:10

We can rejoice in our suffering, not for the pain but for what the hardship produces. When our kids hurt, we hope they seek God's comfort. When they feel alone, we want them to know God is with them. And when they are broken and depleted we pray they ask God for His strength. By teaching our kids these three biblical truths: suffering is temporary, God is near, and God will strengthen us, we raise our children to embrace a God-dependence.

> *Praise be to the God and Father of our Lord Jesus Christ, the Father of compassion and the God of all comfort, who comforts us in all our troubles, so that we can comfort those in any trouble with the comfort we ourselves receive from God. —2 Corinthians 1:3–4*

SHARE THE SAD

When Roni Wing Lambrecht's son Dalton died at 15, she experienced what therapists identify as one of the most devastating losses a parent can face: the death of a child.

"Loneliness was everywhere, even in my husband's embrace. Even now, a few years after losing our son, I often feel isolated. This lessened a bit once I decided to use my pain as a teacher. I began posting on social media the emotional, mental, and physical struggles my husband and I faced. Instead of a Christmas letter, I wrote a grief letter that explained the details of our new existence.

"I was stuck. I read grief books and talked to grief counselors and focused only on my grief. Once I realized I was in a black hole, I made the decision to climb out and fix my thoughts on my blessings. Every day I chose to focus on one good memory of my son.

"The healing began when I got busy and concentrated on someone other than myself. My husband and I have found purpose by starting a Pay It Forward Campaign in our son's memory (more than 3,500 people have now been touched by a random act of kindness). This led me to write three books to help parents cherish small moments with their children, no matter the child's age."

Roni says she is thankful for the time she had with her son. She reflects that many people never even have the opportunity to love so deeply. That kind of love was and is a true gift.

Emotional suffering can cause us to retreat and separate from others. We feel alone when we grieve. Reaching out in the grief, like Roni did, is a way to channel pain in a more positive direction. On the flip side, tenderness and awareness of another person's hurt can also break the grief isolation.

At fourteen, my daughter Kendra received devastating news while on vacation at our family cabin in Minnesota. Her friend was killed in a car accident on the way back to Colorado from Wyoming. She had been on a mission trip.

The family cabin is a busy place. It holds four families plus six dogs. There is so much commotion that some things go unnoticed. Most of the family was unaware of the information Kendra received. Shelley, Kendra's aunt, noticed Kendra was absent from some of the family activities. She searched for her and found her alone, crying in the lower level of the cabin. Shelley sat down beside her niece and gave her a hug.

In the midst of the family craziness, Shelley sought out her missing niece. Presence and a hug were what Kendra needed. Her aunt innately knew this and acted on it. It has been almost ten years since then and Kendra still talks about the love and kindness Auntie Shelley showed her in that moment.

Life is full of stuff—good and bad. To share in all the important parts of life we must teach our kids to lament, show compassion, share the sad, celebrate together, and have a sense of humor. When we do this we are free to be who God created us to be.

BITTER BARRIER

Grief doesn't have to isolate individuals or divide families. But bitterness, resentment, and rebellion take division seriously. They are relationship busters. Unknowingly, some of the actions parents take result in growing the attitudes we do not want to instill.

The best-bud parent is overindulgent, unable to make a decision, pleads and begs, and is overly permissive. His or her goal is to make the child happy and says yes to every material item and whim under the sun. The child never has to earn anything and doesn't experience the chance to say, "Yes, I worked for that."

An indecisive parent appears weak and is unable to lead. A conversation may sound like this, "I don't know. What do you want?" It's OK to have an opinion. Kids need a strong leader who knows when to say yes and when to say no.

Kids do not want a wimpy, pushover parent, one who attempts to cajole with a whimper and a whine, "Please, please, please take out the garbage." Or who cries, "Oh, can't you help me? I'm soooo tired." Be the parent and state what is needed or expected and when it is to be accomplished. Be clear and specific when giving direction. "Take the garbage out before you go to your friend's house." "I need your help with the dishes. Clear the table and put the dishes in the dishwasher after dinner." When expectations are clearly stated there is no room for confusion. Children are more likely to cooperate if they know what it is expected. Parental respect is fostered and a sense of security is grown when we come from a place of strength not fear.

The child's feeling of security bottoms out with the overly permissive mom or dad. These parents appear weak and don't want conflict. They hope by avoiding altercation they can build a stronger relationship. You may hear these words, "Oh, I don't want my child to hate me." But this approach results in resentment and the child feeling unloved. A question that begins to take shape in the child's mind is, "Don't you care enough about me to say no?"

Resentment seeps into a child's heart when the parent is emotionally absent, physically distant, uninformed, or punishes harshly or wrongly. An uninformed parent appears disinterested. Remember your child's friend's names, be able to name their favorite band or singer, and know their go-to fast food order. Be a student of your child.

It is challenging to keep up with the child's changing preferences. Every Christmas I would purchase a calendar for each of my four kids. I chose the individual calendars according to their interests: Bible verses, hockey themes, pug photos, and horse pictures. After opening the horse calendar, my daughter announced, "You always get me a horse calendar. I haven't liked horses for a couple years now. I like beaches." I blew it. I was still catering to her childish preference and overlooked the fact that she had outgrown horses. She was a teen, no longer a tween, and I had missed it.

The opposite of an underinvolved or solicitant parent is the parent who is overly authoritative. When punishment goes too far, seething anger brews inside a child's heart. This anger often turns into rebellion—the very thing the highly controlling parent is hoping to avoid. Avoid delivering consequences when angry. Start small; you can always go bigger later if necessary.

The idea of innocent until proven guilty is a good one. Ask, don't assume or accuse. If you accuse your child of wrongdoing, be accurate. One time my husband and I accused our son of intentionally omitting some important information. As it turned out, we were wrong. He's forgiven us, but he sure hasn't forgotten the incident. (I still feel horrible about it.)

Resentment and rebellion are built over time with repeated patterns. Perhaps like me you have done some of these things. The good news is God can turn any of these relationship issues around. I have learned I need to be aware of my weak areas and ask for forgiveness when I don't react well.

Fathers, do not embitter your children, or they will become discouraged. —Colossians 3:21

A PROFESSIONAL WEDGE

Awareness of our own weak areas is critical. It is equally important to be tuned into our children's issues. We need to be responsive to our kids when struggles come. Sometimes professional help is necessary. According to the National Institute of Mental Health, 30 percent of young adults between the ages of eighteen and twenty-nine suffer with anxiety disorder. Of that 30 percent, less than 37 percent are receiving treatment.

When mental health issues begin to impede responsible everyday life, help needs to be sought. Choosing the best counselor is critical. Jill shares the importance of being attentive and proactive when the sessions prove to be more harmful than helpful.

"Our twenty-one-year-old daughter Jessica struggles with mental health challenges. She is bright and capable, but several bouts of major depression and ongoing anxiety have taken their toll. Jessica deals with high levels of fatigue and poor motivation. It has been difficult for her to continue with school, hold a job, and adequately care for herself. Currently, Jessica is living at home with her dad and me.

"Jessica's most recent counselor was somewhat effective in helping her manage her illness. But we started to notice he was driving a wedge between her and us. When she was unhappy with something we did or said, he validated her, agreed we were being unreasonable, and suggested our parenting was a causative factor in her illness.

"Simultaneously, he told my husband and me, 'Jessica is not taking individual responsibility for her behaviors. She blames her problems on you and others. I urge you to establish age appropriate expectations, set firm boundaries, and reduce monetary support.'

"The hoped-for outcome was for Jessica to recognize her maladaptive behaviors and be motivated to make the necessary changes. The result of following through with this advice was increased emotional distance between us. Jessica's dad and I wanted to deal with this polarization constructively, but the counselor was not comfortable providing family therapy.

"'Mom, it seems like it is me versus you guys. Why don't we work together as a team?' Jessica noticed the distance between us as well.

"With tears I agreed. The counselor's style seemed to pit us against each other. We decided to work together and stop this tug of war. The three of us formed Team Butterfly.

"We no longer use the counselor who created the wedge. As Team Butterfly we have decided to seek another professional who will work with all of us. John and I want to support Jessica's quest to heal, cope, and move forward. In the meantime, we are cheering her on as she takes clearly defined steps toward wellness and self-responsibility.

"The three of us now share a greater level of trust through interdependency. This is much more positive. The other approach had become negative and separated us. Blame rather than solutions was the result. We hope to be part of our daughter's healing process, to help her rather than enable dependency."

The experiences of rivalry and grief and feelings of resentment, bitterness, and blame all have potential to separate us, isolate us, or put a barrier between us. It is good to be aware of the potential harm that can be caused by these feelings and do what we can to prevent a wall from being built in our relationships.

By not rescuing our kids and not solving their problems but instead allowing them to feel sadness, disappointment, discouragement, and grief, we give our kids a gift, the gift of resiliency, tenderness, understanding, and empathy. All these things are learned through personal struggle or even loss.

*They are joined fast to one another; they cling together
and cannot be parted. —Job 41:17*

CHAPTER 8

THE ALL-ABOUT-ME DISCONNECT

*Be devoted to one another in love. Honor one another
above yourselves. —Romans 12:10*

After I concluded my talk to a group of women, I sat next to a mom
holding her little one on her lap. Part of my message was about raising
responsible rather than independent children.

"Can you describe what that looks like now that you are an
adult?" This early thirtysomething mama told me, "I was raised to be
independent." I asked her to unpack what independence looked like in
her family of origin.

"If something goes wrong, I figure it out. I would never call my
parents for help. It's not like I'm hiding something from them, I would
just be more inclined to tell them after the issue is resolved. Maybe this
is the reason why I don't feel especially close to my mom and dad."
She glanced at her little one perched on her lap, "I get it. I want my
daughter to be responsible, but I don't think I really want her to be
independent. That would break my heart."

Independence is linked to entitlement. These two seemingly opposing attitudes are linked through a perspective that says, "It's all about
me."

The independent familial pattern this young mom grew up with
isn't one she wants to pass along. She desires to have her child and
future children to share their lives with her. She is breaking the family
independence mold and creating a new cast of interdependence.

Selfishness is excessively or even exclusively concerned with one's
own advantage without considering others. Both independent people
and entitled individuals look in the mirror and see the only person to
consider is looking right back at them.

BREAK UP WITH INDEPENDENCE

Most moms and dads want to have a relationship with their adult children, one that includes leaning on each other and celebrating together. A natural result of independence, however, is separation. Once we realize what independence really is, most of us don't want it.

What we really want is to raise responsible people—those who care for others, answer for their own conduct, fulfill obligations, keep promises, and are accountable for actions, words, and choices.

Responsibility, trustworthiness, and respect go together. We had four rules in our home: respect others, respect stuff, respect yourself, and respect God. When we act in respectful ways we demonstrate responsibility and cultivate trust.

My friend, counselor Lucille Zimmerman, reminds her clients of psychologist and TV host Dr. Phil's Life Law #8: "We teach people how to treat us." This equips those in her care to expect respect. If we want respect to reign in our home, it starts with mom and dad. We talk and act respectfully. We train our kids to be respectful when we model and expect respect, "I treat you with respect. I expect respect in return."

Responsible people are typically rational people. They can self-regulate and are respectful of others and of themselves. Self-control is a learned behavior where feelings are felt and acknowledged while behavior is thought through before acted out.

To function as a healthy interdependent connected family, members need skills that stem from respectfulness and responsibility. The ability to identify feelings, name them, and express them with I statements such as, "I feel frustrated when dishes are left in the sink," are ways to resolve problems more easily.

"You left the dishes in the sink again. I will just wash them," *sigh*. This could be an indication of a dependent or enabled relationship. Interdependence doesn't enable. Interdependence empowers. It sounds a little different, "I see the dishes in the sink. I am happy to wash them since I have time and you are running late." It is a two-way relationship, where both parties support and show grace.

THE LAUNCH

Eventually we release our kiddos into the world. So our task is really to raise adults. We hope our kids launch well and are prepared to "adult." That step doesn't have to be a giant leap. As our kids grow we can equip them and give them practice in the areas of finance, relationships, and job challenges. Our young people will need to figure out how to grow spiritually, manage their schedule, and maintain good health. We can encourage, nurture, challenge, show compassion, train, and support them in their efforts to move into adulthood.

When our children recognize we have confidence in their ability to handle challenges, they will develop self-confidence and have the mindset to persevere. If they believe they are loved by us and by God—simply because of their intrinsic value and not because of their performance—they will have the courage to risk failure and take the needed time to refine their skills in order to become proficient and capable in tackling problems.

For our kids to succeed at adulting we must allow them to be responsible for their behavior and words and to own their failures, struggles, and disappointments. We hope that in the midst of adulting they don't just scrape by on survival-of-the-fittest skills but actually thrive by becoming the people God has created them to be, people who pursue their passion and God's call on their life.

SINGLE STATUS

Typically adulting begins when an individual is post high school and single. Paula, a young single woman in her early thirties, describes what she has learned about independence and being single.

"I used to pride myself on being independent. When I was a kid, my dad would take my brother and me to wrestling matches. I would go off by myself—perfectly content to do my own thing. As I got older, I made my own way: moved away from my hometown, paid for my own car, pursued higher education, and got my own apartment. I didn't need anyone and didn't want to need anyone. In my singleness God has shown me this isn't how He wants me to be. This past year I have had some extreme health issues, and I've been unable to drive or work. I must rely on other people to take me to church, to the grocery store, and to my doctor appointments. I realize I crave companionship and friendship. During this season of my life, I have learned I must proactively reach out to others, ask for help when necessary, and accept help when offered. I think independence is closely tied to pride. God wants us to rely on Him and on other people."

Dale Wilsher, life coach and single mom, would agree with Paula's assessment and would add that a village is needed.

In her 1corinthians13parenting.com blog post, "Does it have to take a village?" she says, "I'm a self-sufficient kind of gal and I come from a long line of hard working self-sustaining people. I remember hearing my parents talk about the phrase, 'It takes a village to raise a child' as if it were heresy. Back then it had a political meaning they didn't support, but I took it to mean that I should never need emotional, spiritual, or practical help as a parent, and if I did, I must be doing something wrong. . . . When my children were small, [I was able to maintain] my independence [while I managed to take care of my family's needs].

"But now as a single mom, it's ridiculous how much help I need. I've needed friends to take my children overnight when I've had to go out of town. I've needed my children to drive each other to work when my schedule wouldn't allow me to drive. I've needed the bus to take my children to and from school. I've needed my neighbor to let my dog in when we forgot and left her out. That one is always embarrassing. I've needed my parents, aunts, and uncles to help with my oldest daughter in college because she is 1,400 miles away. I've needed youth leaders to teach my children and connect with them in ways I am not able. That is just the tip of the iceberg.

"I used to be the mom with the giant SUV who could transport gaggles of children in carpool. I used to be the mom who hosted youth group meetings, giant sleepovers, and fun parties. I used to be the mom who cooked dinner every night. I used to be the mom with a cleaner house. I used to be the mom who prayed with her kids every night. I used to be and do a lot of things. I felt successful because I didn't need much help from other parents. I had my life together. I had no need of a village.

"Today I need a village because I need help. And I am grateful for all the help I have received, but I rarely get to pay those parents back. There is nothing more humbling than receiving a gift that you can never repay. [My village doesn't] have the same needs as I do, so for now they don't need me . . . but I need them. Village life is the way the Christian life is meant to be lived.

"God put us in a body of believers so that the foot could need the hand and the eye could need the nose. We were never designed to be all the parts. We need each other's skills, strengths, and gifts. We were designed to live in a village, connected to each other and connected to God. This keeps us out of isolation and loneliness while it gives us a place to belong."

This passage from Romans reminds us how we are created to depend on each other.

> For just as each of us has one body with many members, and these members do not all have the same function, so in Christ we, though many, form one body, and each member belongs to all the others.
> —Romans 12:4–5

ENTITLED EXPECTATIONS

Collectively we parents need to take some responsibility for raising entitled kids. We have participated in creating an entitlement attitude. We train our kids to have unrealistic expectations. We encourage them to think they are so great at . . . everything. We teach them if they want it, they will achieve it. We say things like:

"You deserve better."

"He's not good enough for you."

"You are the [smartest, cutest, strongest] person I know."

OK, let's get real. No one can be the best at everything. And in regard to value, no one person is better or worse than another. We are all equal at the foot of the Cross.

The idea of "I deserve" in the sense of global fairness is an entitled thought. This type of fairness doesn't include result, effort, or outcome. "Because I breathe like he does, I deserve a posh job."

Entitlement plays out in the classroom as well. Parents are often active participants.

"You gave my child a D. He's trying to get into [fill in the blank] college. He needs at least a B."

Mrs. Nash, a middle school teacher, has developed a great line she uses when parents want her to change a grade, "I don't give grades. My students earn grades." She puts the responsibility back on the child, where it belongs.

When I taught third grade I recall one conference where the parent demanded her daughter be placed in the highest level math group (even though the student's ability in math was average). The mom reasoned that her child needed to be moved up a level so she would qualify for the better programs offered at the middle school and high school level.

There are parents who have a vision for who their child ought to be and the path necessary for them to get there. The dream supersedes the reality. Sometimes teachers and grades are viewed as obstacles to remove rather than hills to conquer. Parents want the best yet don't train the child to work for it. The train of thought is dream it and it will happen. For dreams to become a reality, effort and perseverance are typically part of the package. There are times the parent's expectations don't match the child's abilities.

We feel disappointed when our hopes don't come to fruition and we feel badly when our child's dreams are dashed. Sympathy is a voice that can promote dependency. It kicks responsibility to the curb and allows blame to move in. Dependency is closely linked to entitlement. In an attempt to encourage our kids when things don't work out the way they had hoped, we may say things like:

"You deserved to get that part."

"Do whatever you need to get ahead."

"The failure wasn't your fault."

"You should have received all the credit."

Entitled thoughts are generated when the above statements are received and believed:

"I deserve better."

"The world owes me."

"Failure is someone else's fault."

"I'm more important than anyone else in the room."

Struggle is a good character builder. Hardship builds empathy, encourages humility, and strengthens perseverance. Difficulties create opportunities to problem solve, be stretched, and be creative.

If we want to empower our kids we will encourage them in the difficult places and allow the struggle to play out. We can sit alongside them in the disappointment. We can say things like:

"I know you wanted that part in the play. I'm sorry that didn't work out."

"Always demonstrate respect for others and personal integrity."

"When we fail, it's no big deal. We learn from that and figure out another way to do something."

"Sharing credit with others is an honorable thing to do,"

When these things are spoken the child comes to understand:

"Everybody struggles with something."

"I am created on purpose for a purpose. I can contribute to the world."

"My successes and my failures are mine alone."

"We are all equal at the foot of the Cross."

In an empowered place, our kids experience both defeat and victory with an adjusted mindset. They realize ups and downs are a part of life. When they come to terms with this reality, contentment is found and thankfulness and gratefulness have a place to blossom. The muscles of tenacity and perseverance are able to bulk up. Even if their experiences contain disappointment, life can be viewed through a wider lens. In 1 Thessalonians 5:18 Paul bids believers to, "Give thanks in all circumstances, for this is God's will for you in Christ Jesus."

AFFLUENZA AFFLICTION

When we empower our kids we prevent undeserved privilege and inoculate against spoiled and self-centered children. We work from the end backward. Start by asking, "What do I want my kids to develop?" Most parents want their children to have a good work ethic along with a good attitude (even when things don't go well). We hope to raise unselfish, grateful, and responsible self-starters.

Retraining is called for. We can get back to the old school idea of merited compensation, the idea of putting forth effort, striving to do well, and having a thankful heart. We fight the entitlement mentality when we compliment when it is warranted, show appreciation for family members, assign household chores, give children an honest perspective of themselves, and empower them with ownership. These methods provide opportunities to develop responsibility and interdependency among all family members.

When our kids have some skin in the game, they gain a sense of control and personal responsibility for an outcome. They are motivated to take a positive action rather than passively wait for things to happen. This will extinguish the victim or blame mentality held by an entitled individual.

When struggle occurs, let's change our language. Rather than say, "You deserve," say, "How will you accomplish your goal?" or, "What goals have you set to reach your desired outcome?"

When you hear, "I want," "I need," or "I deserve," help your child reframe their thoughts to, "I will do this," "I will not do that," or "I'm responsible for." A child who seeks to blame others for their own failures or looks to others to provide health, wealth, and happiness is likely to be a very unhappy and unproductive person.

Parents set the tone in the home. We can choose to be positive or negative. Model a good attitude regarding struggles, inconveniences, and chores. "The cleaning needs to get done, and I am so thankful I have a house to clean." Talk about the silver lining in your challenges. Discuss how the difficulties and struggles are the best teachers.

The parenting philosophy of independence has the potential to breed selfishness. An independent individual looks out only for the best interest of oneself. Interdependency moves us to unselfishness and connects us to our family and to others.

ENTITLEMENT DEPENDENCY

Selflessness is a godly characteristic. Having a job or taking responsibility is also a biblical principle. Scripture reinforces the idea that work is honorable and an important part of being a human.

Genesis 2 demonstrates God's design for work and personal responsibility:

> The LORD God took the man and put him in the Garden of Eden to work it and take care of it. —Genesis 2:15

> Now the LORD God had formed out of the ground all the wild animals and all the birds in the sky. He brought them to the man to see what he would name them; and whatever the man called each living creature, that was its name. So the man gave names to all the livestock, the birds in the sky and all the wild animals. —Genesis 2:19–20

In the New Testament, Paul states he was not financially dependent upon others for his ministry. He contributed to the community through his preaching and his tent-making job (Acts 18:1–4; 1 Thessalonians 2:9).

Work is a good and godly practice. It can bring fulfillment, satisfaction, and a sense of accomplishment. Working with others, like Paul and his tentmaker and ministry friends Aquila and Priscilla, encourages a spirit of interdependency.

Scripture also talks about our attitude toward work. We could even expand it to changing diapers, carpooling, and making meals. We can do our work, whatever our vocation or situation, to the glory of God. Colossians 3:23 helps us to refocus.

> *Whatever you do, work at it with all your heart, as working for the Lord, not for human masters.*

Between bites of pizza Tom told me a story of a young man who decided work wasn't his thing. Tom described what was seen on the strategically placed security camera at his place of employment. The camera caught the guy clocking in, going out the backdoor, climbing the fence, and then returning at the end of the day to clock out." This was a daily pattern for the now former employee. The young man collected a paycheck but definitely did not earn one.

Work isn't a curse. The concept of work came before the fall in Genesis 3. Adam was given the jobs of caring for God's creation and naming the animals—prior to the fall. Those jobs were part of Adam's purpose. Work is good.

PLENTY PROBLEMS

Paul was clear about his purpose—proclaiming Jesus to the world. But he did not have it easy. As Paul worked out his mission he experienced much suffering, yet he was content in his circumstances. He found satisfaction in his dependent relationship with the Lord. "I know what it is to be in need, and I know what it is to have plenty. I have learned the secret of being content in any and every situation, whether well fed or hungry, whether living in plenty or in want. I can do all this through him who gives me strength" (Philippians 4:12–13).

Wise moms and dads do not give their children everything they want. If they do provide for every whim, the entitlement attitude is birthed and the problem of plenty sets in. Not giving our children everything their hearts desire is an everlasting gift. Another present kids can receive from their parents is the opportunity to work for some things.

We love to give good gifts. So does God. In Matthew 7:11 it says, "If you, then, though you are evil, know how to give good gifts to your children, how much more will your Father in heaven give good gifts to those who ask him!" Not all gifts are material, some are character building. The gifts of kindness, a smile, and the present of presence are treasures.

Pride is one of those qualities that taints a good gift. It comes in the form of comparison—"I'm better than you," or, "My [car, house, job, family] is better than yours." It has been said by many theologians that pride is the root of all sin. Pride over possessions, power, or prestige blocks our view. It is hard to see others when our lenses are fixed on ourselves and our wants. When we lend a hand to a single parent or work with another side-by-side, we understand how destructive independence can be. It gets in the way of caring for others and pushes personal responsibility away. We can choose to live life together so we can say, "I will help you clean it up."

> *Do nothing out of selfish ambition or vain conceit.*
> *Rather, in humility value others above yourselves.*
> *—Philippians 2:3*

CHAPTER 9

THE SYNERGY OF EFFECTIVE LEADERSHIP

For when one says, "I follow Paul," and another, "I follow Apollos," are you not mere human beings? What, after all, is Apollos? And what is Paul? Only servants, through whom you came to believe—as the Lord has assigned to each his task.
—1 Corinthians 3:4–5

The atmosphere was charged with energy. The results were in. My colleagues had just voted to go on strike. The teaching staff was called to a meeting in the school cafeteria. It was my second year as an elementary school teacher. I was just thankful I had a job, while many seasoned tenured teachers were not happy with the compensation.

My school's union representative went over striker protocol.

"You cannot throw things at people or cars but we can get license plate numbers of individuals who cross the picket line so we can harass them."

This was absurd. I was standing in the middle of a group of elementary school teachers who daily managed and prevented difficult student behaviors, trained kids to be kind and not bully, and maintained an environment of respect and safety so learning could occur. Wouldn't the assumption be that professional educators would not throw rocks or other items? And why was it acceptable to harass people?

This leader was not someone I wanted to follow. This was not a movement in which I wanted to participate. I didn't cross the picket line nor did I walk it. I chose to stay home those nine days.

FOLLOW THE LEADER

Most parents would say they want to raise a leader not a follower. We want kids who can lead, have a mind of their own, and are not swayed by peer pressure. However, before our kids can lead they must learn how and who to follow. Being a good follower requires humility and a teachable heart.

Interdependent relationships have leaders and followers. Roles and responsibilities will change depending on the situation, and both positions are valuable and necessary but not equal. An interdependent home doesn't function like a democracy; the parents are still in charge.

When choosing a leader to back or a cause to champion, wisdom and discernment are needed.

People who demonstrate integrity and honesty and who hold similar values and morals as we do are typically good leaders. Good leaders are willing to train, delegate responsibility, be decisive, demonstrate confidence with humility, and effectively communicate their mission with passion and clarity.

We desire to have our children to follow our lead. We ask: Did I act like a leader? Am I training my children to be good followers so they can be effective leaders? Let's do some self-examination by answering these questions:

Do I give my children opportunities to be responsible?

Do my children participate in household chores?

Am I decisive?

Do I demonstrate confidence with humility?

Am I able to effectively communicate my directions and guidance with clarity and passion?

These five questions are indicators of sound leadership. If you answered no to most of these questions, it's possible you feel as though you are a slave to your children's whims and are maybe even fearful of them getting angry with you. Turn things around so you can be the parent in the home by making changes that will bring affirmative responses to the questions.

Before training our kids to lead, we train them to be good followers. Parents are the first leaders children experience. Jesus is our best example of what an effective leader looks like. He had his gang of twelve. Eleven learned what it meant to be a good follower, with Judas as the exception. They were able to go forth and be leaders who trained leaders because they followed well.

We can learn effective follower techniques from these men. These strategies can be applied to growing leadership skills in our children. Accounts in the Gospels point to the apostles' dedication and showed how Jesus trained them to lead. Jesus' approach is a good model for parents who want to raise leaders. The heart qualities the eleven possessed are characteristics for moms and dads to encourage in their children.

In Luke 5:5; 9:1–2; and 19:30–34 we see that the apostles were committed and able to follow directions without being micromanaged by Jesus.

It's up to us to set our kids up for success. And it is easier for children to follow and cooperate if we can be clear in our instructions and then allow them the space to do the task without hovering or redoing. Directives that are short and clear have a better chance of being carried out. Rather than a vague coded message like, "There sure are a lot of dishes in the sink," say, "Put the dishes in the sink into the dishwasher." This grows the leadership qualities of reliability and responsibility.

In Luke 11:1–4; 12:41; and 17:5 the disciples embraced a student-like attitude. Because Jesus was decisive, confident, and humble, He was approachable and respected. His followers wanted to learn from Him, felt comfortable asking questions, and were able to self-advocate. Like the disciples, our children's confidence and knowledge base will grow when they feel secure enough to ask for what they need. There are ways littles can practice self-advocating in a home that feels emotionally safe. For instance, if your young child is fussing say, "Use your words so I know what you need." If the child is older you could say, "You said you were tardy to your first class today. How do you want to solve the problem going forward? Can I help?" These interactions may seem insignificant but are actually quite powerful if you want your child to increase his or her leadership skills while practicing interdependence.

Part of being a learner so one can be a leader is the ability to accept correction. Correcting, not criticizing, goes down much better if the parent or leader provides the adjustment with gentleness and humility. Criticism sounds like, "You did this all wrong. What a huge mess." Instead Jesus used the technique of asking questions in order to correct in Mark 9:33–35. This approach works great with older kids, "What might you do differently next time?" Little ones may need a bit more leading, "Try it this way."

Learning from mistakes is the best teacher. Parents need to let the children know that mistakes are OK and perfection is not expected. Part of being human is figuring out what works and doesn't work. Making mistakes and discovering new and different ways is a lifelong endeavor. If kids are freed from the perfection infection they realize there is no shame in learning via trial and error.

Give your kids opportunities to teach what they have learned. Mentoring and teaching another is a great leadership skill. First as the parent leader, model how this is done. Then provide moments for your kiddos to teach you something.

We lived in San Diego when our kids were little. One of our regular outings was to visit Sea World. These outings stirred the kids' curiosity about the ocean and its inhabitants. I used to tell my extended family who live in Minnesota, "My kids may not know farm animals but they have the sea creatures down." Tom and I learned all about narwhals and whale sharks due to their quest for knowledge. They taught me the difference between a pilot whale and a dolphin. I was able to teach them about farm animals.

Learning and teaching are both good follower and leader skills. Allow your kids to teach you about something they are passionate about. Watching your children light up while teaching you something they have learned brings joy to both parent and child, while strengthening the relationship.

To be an effective leader, being an effective—not perfect—follower comes first. While following Jesus, the disciples observed and learned how to clearly communicate the mission and directions, be approachable and teach, delegate responsibility, provide reassurance, and present opportunities for growth. They functioned like a team and learned how to lead from the best teacher of all.

TEAM SPIRIT

Interdependent connected groups and families function well when the individuals work from their natural abilities and personality types. My husband Tom has an MBA in finance and is a CPA. I squeaked through high school math. Debbie, one of my post-college roommates and a banker, called me "a banker's nightmare." It makes sense for Tom to manage the checkbook.

Depending on the group and activity in which one is involved, sometimes leadership is required and other times following is needed. Throughout life we find ourselves being both leaders and followers.

Laura Crosby perfectly captures how her introverted daughter Katy has been coached through some social situations.

"John and I have two daughters. They are total opposites. Our younger daughter Maggie is a mini-me, able to talk to a fence post and likely to get a response. Our older daughter Katy is more like my husband, introverted. She is a self-described 'policy nerd' who works in DC. The good thing is that these two girls, when they are their best selves, seek to learn from each other and us, their parents. Katy has been known to text Maggie and me and ask for a little coaching on how to connect. We will walk her through specifics of the situation, but most often we remind her, 'Everyone is insecure and unsure of themselves. Find someone who looks uncomfortable and make it your goal to set them at ease. And looking at your phone is off-limits. You've got this!'"

Katy's mom and sister provide practical help and encouragement in situations where she doesn't feel confident. When it comes to social things, Laura or Maggie is likely to take the lead. Katy is comfortable following in those situations because they are not her strength. In turn, Maggie relies on Katy's expertise for things like editing a résumé or becoming familiar with a political situation.

The Crosbys are a great example of an interdependent family. They rely on each other for help and encouragement. Each sister has her own set of natural skills and abilities. Each young woman has something of value to offer the other. They are there for each other.

WATER WALKING

Even if something isn't our strength we can still learn skills to improve or take a risk with things that are not comfortable.

In Matthew 14:25–33 Peter, as a follower, took a risk. He stepped out of the safety of a boat in the middle of a storm to walk toward Jesus. It was a risk worth taking because he trusted his master. Followers who take risks become courageous leaders.

Tom and I went to college in Duluth, Minnesota. Near the campus there was a local swimming hole. Jumping off the cliff was the quickest way to access the refreshing spring-fed water. We took a risk. We weren't reckless; it was a reasonable risk that held a little danger. We felt that adrenaline rush because we met a challenge and conquered some fear.

That adrenaline rush is less appealing as one becomes a parent. Tom and I, along with our two youngest daughters, both twenty-something, visited Canon City, Colorado, one summer. We (and by we, I mean they) decided to go zip lining across the Royal Gorge. I was not about to let my fear get the best of me. I talked myself through it to move my frozen feet up the stairs to the launching deck. "I don't want Samantha and Kendra to think I'm a wimp." The twentysome-thing male attendants suppressed their laughter and securely buckled me in. I sailed over the Arkansas River at 1,200 feet. I clenched the cable with an iron grip, just in case the seat decided to drop out from under me. My fear almost prevented the thrill. It could have robbed me of a memory with my family. The fingernail dents and the rope burn on my palms lasted the rest of the day. They served as a reminder that I overcame my fear. Now I can cross the Royal Gorge zip line off my bucket list.

Parents, we have become risk averse. Risk aversion takes away the moments that build courage and bravery. If we want to raise a leader, our kiddos need to experience conquering fear by taking a chance and depending on God. Allow for adventure and the possibility of failure while of course steering away from situations that are reckless, careless, or immoral. Encourage the "Let's give it a shot" and the "It's OK even if it's not done perfectly" mentalities. Build character by allowing for some risks; this will increase your child's confidence and competence.

When we let our children take a risk and have that experience of conquering fear, they discover who they are, know what they believe, and increase their dependence on the Father. The goal is to be who God created us to be. Part of achieving that aim includes conquering our fear and stepping out of the boat (or zip lining over the Royal Gorge). Faith isn't fearless. Faith is fear conquered. Support an adventurous spirit as long as it remains in line with glorifying God.

Passion is the fuel that drives purpose. For our kids to discover who God designed them to be, they must unearth their passion. Matt Thomas, president and cofounder of Expedition Backcountry Adventures, says that raising passionate young people begins with the parents.

In his 1corinthians13parenting.com blog post, "Raising Passionate Young People," he says, "I remember sitting down in my office with a couple concerned that their sixteen-year-old son was going nowhere. They used the word *apathetic* as a descriptor several times throughout our conversation. 'He doesn't do anything but sit in his room and play video games,' they lamented. 'We're concerned about his future, and we just want him to care about *something*!'

"Curious, I asked Dad what his evening routine was like when he came home from work. He said, 'I typically make it home for dinner, then once the little one is down I watch Sportscenter . . . twice.'

"I asked Mom the same thing and she responded, 'Well, after dinner is finished I make lunches for the kids and then cozy up with my iPad to peruse Facebook and Pinterest.'

"'Hmm. What about the weekends?' I asked.

"They looked at each other nervously and began to share a typical laundry list of suburban weekend activities: yard work, golf, grocery shopping, church, television, etc. Rinse and repeat fifty-two weeks out of the year.

"I concluded our time with a simple question for this couple, 'What in your life inspires your kids to live with purpose and passion?'

"All too often we blame the culture for our children's apathy. We point to music, film, and public school as the guilty parties in our teenager's seemingly disengaged disposition. Sure, popular culture has great influence on our young people but lest we forget, so do we.

"Teenagers watch their parents' every move. . . . They are paying attention, and how you live has greater impact on your young ones than what you say ever could."

Here are some tips for raising kids who are passionately purpose driven.

Avoid rescuing: Allow for failure and the learning that accompanies it. Successful people fail well. They fall, pick themselves up again, brush off the dust, and try a new way.

Avoid being uber-realistic: Let your kids dream and pursue a passion. Be a support and assist in bringing those ideas to fruition. Avoid rewarding for the sole purpose of being fair. Rewards are earned.

Avoid removing obstacles for your children: Let them jump the hurdle, deal with difficulty, and take responsibility for an undesirable outcome.

Avoid focusing solely on results: Performance plus perseverance matters. Character is often built in times of failure.

Avoid speaking for your child when they can advocate for themselves: Train him or her in how to ask for help when assistance or support is needed.

Avoid excessive screen time: Excessive screen time interferes with the time it takes and the personal interaction necessary to develop the soft skills of building relationships, effectively communicating, and maturing conflict resolution.

Avoid taking over or micromanaging: Train your children to perform tasks so they can gain confidence and proficiency.

Avoid squelching their ideas: Be a support, and assist in bringing those ideas to fruition.

Avoid complacency: Show your children how passionate participation in a cause you care about can effect change. When you do this your children are more likely to do the same.

These tips are good guidelines to follow if we want to raise a passionate, purpose-filled person. If we are serious about raising this type of individual, we must be passionate and purpose-filled parents.

PEACE OUT

The passions our kids hold can be smothered by a culture that continually challenges and bombards their belief systems. We need to arm our kids with the tools they need to be leaders. My friend and fellow mentor mom from The Mom Initiative, Julie Sanders, wrote an article, "Raising kids with the urge to lead," in which she encourages parents to resist the urge to rescue or interfere but instead build strength and perseverance. Encourage, model, and pray for your child's leadership skills to provide guidance and motivation.

Society encourages our kids to be peacekeepers rather than peacemakers. But our kids need the tools to be a peacemaker. A peacemaker doesn't sit idly by, hoping no one will get upset or feel challenged. A peacemaker changes the status quo with love and truth. Jesus, the Prince of Peace says, "Blessed are the peacemakers for they will be called children of God" (Matthew 5:9).

Have you ever compared the words, *make* and *keep*? Perhaps these words have been milling around in my mind because I need to know how the Lord wants me to proceed in a difficult situation. (Of course I want to keep the peace—but in doing so, is there a cost?) I desire to demonstrate God's love, peace, truth, mercy, justice, and compassion. How can this be done in the midst of a potentially contentious struggle?

Our kids need to be prepared for the times they need to step up to the plate and stand up to a bully on another's behalf or speak up when injustice is present. Peacemaking is a leadership skill to be developed in both parents and kids.

As a society, we have become confused by what peace looks like and how we achieve it. We believe peace is being quiet and not rocking the boat. Jesus was not a peace keeper. He stirred things up according to what was right, just, and loving.

I did a little exercise and contrasted the words, *keep* and *make*.

Peacekeeper	Peacemaker
Place of Weakness	Place of Strength
Motivated by Fear	Motivated by Faith
Passive	Proactive
Pacify	Protect, Defend
Tolerates Injustice	Stands Up to Injustice
Status Quo	Change
Looks the Other Way	Engages
Rolls Over	Stands Up
Values Silence	Values Speaking Up
Conforms	Transforms

When we keep, we are holding on, maintaining, refraining, and conforming. When we make, we are shaping, creating, causing, changing, and transforming.

Mercy and justice, grace and truth are values to be held in proper tension. Let your communication be seasoned with humility and laced with strength so your home is a place where peace is made.

MAKE PEACE

"Do something!" The woman, lying prostrate on the floor, implores a man in uniform to help as armed men take over a bank.

"I'm not a security guard. I'm a security *monitor*," he responds. "I only notify people if there is a robbery."

The monitor looks around and says, "There's a robbery."

This commercial for LifeLock, a company that helps monitor and address identity theft, speaks a profound message. None of us only wants to know there is a problem; we want help to fix it. The knowledge and the solution demonstrate the difference between peace keepers and peace makers. A peace keeper, like the security monitor, really doesn't get involved in any solution. A peace maker takes action, like a security guard.

"Just get along." "Just let your little brother tag along." "Just behave." "Just be nice." Those are statements spoken by peace keeping parents. Nothing changes. The problem isn't solved, it's only acknowledged. "Just" isn't an effective way to resolve a problem.

Peace making requires a little bravery and a big commitment. Whenever I feel fear, rather than rely on faith, I realize I am falling into peace keeping mode. Conflict is uncomfortable. I fear loss of a relationship or I worry someone won't like me. I want everyone to be OK. I am beginning to learn (admittedly this is still hard for me) to fight my natural inclination to step in and smooth things over.

Sometimes being a peace maker is moving out of God's way and not rescuing. Jesus, the Prince of peace, was committed to doing things God's way. He was motivated by faith (Luke 22:42), was proactive (Luke 6), stood up to injustice (John 2:12–17), and valued transformation (John 3:1–8). Jesus was not a peace keeper, He was a peace maker.

LEADERS ARE DECISION MAKERS

Have you called out these lines as your child walked out the door?

Make good choices.

Be smart.

WWJD (What would Jesus do)?

Remember who you are.

If all your friends jumped off a bridge, would you too?

Remember to whom you belong.

Drive safe.

These are all questions or statements parents make to encourage their kids to think before they act. I've said most of them. Honestly, they weren't all that effective. Parents talk and kids hear, "Blah, blah, blah." Then respond with, "Yeah, yeah, I know."

The trouble with all these go-to words of advice is that they are nonspecific and difficult to apply in the middle of a decision or crisis. They also come out of the parent's mouth rather than the child's head. What if we instead trained our kiddos to strain their decision making through the Philippians 4 filter?

> *Whatever is true, whatever is noble, whatever is right, whatever is pure, whatever is lovely, whatever is admirable—if anything is excellent or praiseworthy —think about such things. Whatever you have learned or received or heard from me, or seen in me—put into practice. And the God of peace will be with you.*
> *—Philippians 4:8–9*

Paul tells us to put what we have learned into practice. Here's a way we can apply these verses. Take the qualities Paul mentions and craft them into questions to determine a yes or no answer. This raises the bar from, "Should I or shouldn't I?" to "Whatever I have learned, am I putting it into practice?" Questions move us to think. When using the Philippians verse for decision making we utilize the "whatevers" and turn them into questions. The whatever questions steer our kids and us to discover:

Is it true?

Is it noble?

Is it right?

Is it pure?

Is it lovely?

Is it admirable?

Is it excellent?

Is it praiseworthy?

Does this line up with what I have learned or received or heard or seen in God's Word?

The answers to the whatevers are the should-or-should-not plumb line for our wonderings. Asking the questions and finding the answers take us from the independent thinking mode and scoot us over to a God dependency. Faithful moms and dads want to be in God's will. We hope our children will desire the same thing. If we ask ourselves and train our kids to ask and respond to the Philippians 4 whatevers, God promises His peace.

Affirmative answers to all the whatever questions will clear the confusion and bring peace and confidence in the big and small decisions. The decision is clear and simple. (But that doesn't mean when it is played out it will be easy.)

We can't always be with our kids. Even if it is our heart's desire to be the one who comes alongside to help clean up the spill, we want them to rely on the Lord so they are able to speak, think, reason, and act with wisdom and embrace a God dependence.

> *Remember your leaders, who spoke the word of God to you. Consider the outcome of their way of life and imitate their faith.* —Hebrews 13:7

CHAPTER 10

MAKE NECESSARY ADJUSTMENTS

Therefore let us stop passing judgment on one another. Instead, make up your mind not to put any stumbling block or obstacle in the way of a brother or sister. —Romans 14:13

I found a new path today. The gray gravel took me through trees and shrubs along a creek to an overlook. I chose to walk in a different direction because I have to figure out my new normal. My sweet Murphy boy, the best dog ever, died just three days ago. He was my walking and hiking companion. As he became an older gentleman our walks were shorter and our hikes less strenuous. My sister suggested, "Lor, take a new route. It will be easier on your heart." Loss or change isn't easy. Sometimes it's downright agonizing.

It can be hard to deal in reality to accept the unacceptable, navigate the unexpected, and adjust course. Our role or life situation never remains stagnant. Change is a constant. We need to learn to readjust or reconnect due to our circumstances.

Being a single parent, a stepparent, a grandparent, or an in-law requires a role adjustment. To maintain relationship we need to be flexible. To thrive together we must let go of our vision, deal in reality, and seek to glorify God in the midst.

SINGLE SETTING

Single parents have a challenge before them—to connect even when their child isn't with them. I'm not a single parent, so I looked to my friend and colleague, Matt Haviland, from A Father's Walk, a single dads ministry, who wrote a blog post, "Single Dad, You Can Still Be

Dad!" for 1corinthians13parenting.com. His message can be applied to single moms too.

"'Single dad' doesn't always mean you have your kids full time; and even if you are the primary caregiver, there are still bound to be times when you are apart from each other for longer periods. I recently had a new single father describe being apart from his children like 'a hole in my gut.' . . .

"There is no distance, circumstance, or hindrance that prevents you from praying for your children—except yourself. The Bible is very clear that prayer works. I cannot think of many things greater than a father praying for his children.

"If it's an option, use the technology we have to reach out to your children, and leave for the better after they have talked with you (this may mean holding some emotions back during your talk). Be available, as much as you can for them to call you too. Let them know their time is always cherished. . . .

"I have been keeping a journal for years for my daughter, and I hope to present all of my writings to her one day when she is older. Begin now writing down the memories you have already created with them and write words of love and affirmation while you are apart. This will be a living message they can hold on to long after we are gone. . . .

"Make your house a home. Clean up if need be, and maybe surprise [the kids] by adding some fresh paint to their room, rearranging or creating a new play area, or anything else that sends a surprise message of love once they are back.

"There is no greater use of your time apart from your children than to work on your own personal relationship with the Lord and growing as a man, father, and leader. Dive into the Word and seek His guidance. Improve and grow your prayer life. Make any changes in the natural and spiritual that will help you leave a legacy that honors God and impacts your son or daughter for His purposes."

Matt has a prayer he has written for single parents, which is found in his 1corinthians13parenting.com blog post, "A Single Parent's Prayer."

Father,

I come before You today broken, yet humbled. Thank You, my Lord, for another opportunity to serve You; and although my circumstances may be far from ideal right now, they could not be in more perfect hands than Yours. Jesus, You call for all of us who are weary and heavy laden to come before You and that You will give us rest. God, my body and my soul both need rest right now. There are days I feel like nothing is going right; other days I am irritated and stressed beyond what it seems I can handle. There are times I wonder how I am ever going to make it on the path You have laid out before me. But then I reflect upon Your promises for my life. You have promised to never leave me or forsake me and that every good gift is from above. I believe Jesus has been tried and tempted in every way I have and that I can do all things through Him who strengthens me. And for that today, Lord, I am grateful.

Father, please help me to have a softened heart toward my children's father/mother. Lord, please forgive me for when I have acted out toward him/her when I shouldn't have. God, help me to remember that I am just as broken as they are and that Jesus died for him/her the same as He died for me. God, I pray You would bless my children's father/mother, that You would draw his/her heart toward Yours and that You would keep him/her safe and healthy. Lord, help me to have an attitude of forgiveness and to show grace even when it is not being reciprocated back to me. Help me to take the high road and to hold fast to that standard to which I have attained.

Lord, please bless my children. Help me bring them up in Your Word so that even when they are old they will not depart from it. Please protect them both in the natural and the supernatural. I pray to bind the negative influences of this world over their lives and to release Your promises over them instead. Keep them safe and healthy and allow them to be bold witnesses to their friends for Your sake. Above all, my Lord, please continue to change me from glory to glory so that I may be used in a mighty way for Your purposes. Help me to offer my body as a living and holy sacrifice, walking in a way that is pure in every aspect of my life. For I know my eternity is secured in You and that You will supply my every need. Thank You for everything You have blessed me with.

In Jesus' Name,

Amen.

BEST STEPS

Laura grew up in a single parent home. Later, she married into a family that consisted of her husband and his two boys. Laura Petherbridge, also known as the Smart Stepmom, shares her experience and hard-learned connection wisdom in her blog post "On Stepfamily Living: What's a Hill to Die On?" for 1corinthians13parenting.com.

"My husband was a single parent for seven years after his divorce. His eleven- and thirteen-year-old sons thought the four food groups consisted of Pepsi, pizza, hot dogs, and chips. These delicacies were consumed in front of the TV, rarely a fork or spoon in sight.

"I grew up in a single parent home where you sat properly at the table and ate what was on your plate or you went hungry. There was no buffet of choices, and you didn't get a snack later that evening if you didn't finish your dinner.

"In the first few years of being a stepmom I foolishly decided that a major part of my role was to teach my stepsons to eat healthy foods. My motives were right. My methods were wrong. I was on a mission to 'help them' learn how to properly sit at a table, and eat turkey, peas, and mashed potatoes. . . .

"Food became a major battle, and a hill to die on, in an unnecessary war. I was the combat general, who was right. I wanted to prove I was in control of my own home. . . . Everyone was miserable, including my husband. I was viewed as an overbearing tyrant, who bullied the kids and my spouse, not a loving stepmom.

"If the stepchild believes that the stepmom is forcing Dad to set boundaries, it's very likely he/she will resent the stepparent. They will view her as an enforcer and dad as a weakling who buckles under his wife's demands. Stepkids often view a stepparent as an outsider, and this conflict confirms their perspective.

"When I finally raised a white flag of surrender, everyone breathed a sigh of relief. Our mealtimes moved from one of tension and arguing, to times of discussion and fun. I realized I might be winning the battle, but losing the war. My healthy eating efforts as a stepmom created a wall, not a bridge.

"Then God had to help me understand that these innocent young men already had two parents. And I wasn't one of them. If the boys' mom and dad didn't view food as the task to tackle, why was I—the stepmom—turning it into a war?

"Over the years and dealing with stepchildren who lived in two homes there would be many times when taking a strong stand as a stepmom was required. Unlike food, many stepparents face issues such as: disrespect, stealing, lying, domestic violence, drug use, self-harm, and abuse. Those things are a hill to die on and should not be ignored. The parent must be the one to enforce consequences because of the natural bond between parent and child. Although stepparents would like that connection and relationship to be the same, it usually isn't present with a stepparent for a long time. . . .

"Learning what should or should not be a hill to die on is different for each stepfamily. It's not uncommon for the parent to view matters as insignificant, and the stepparent sees them as crucial. This is because parents see their child through the lens of love, and a stepparent sees them through the lens of responsibility. A neutral third party is often needed to help discern the best steps."

Laura mentions parents have a different perspective than a stepparent does. She identified which hills are worth the fight and which ones only cause greater division in a step family. Nuclear families can learn from this too. We ask, "What battles are worth fighting?" The answer usually boils down to issues related to morals, values, and faith.

BRIDGING THE GENERATION GAP

Our nuclear family may be intact or it could be broken. Either way support can be found via the older generation. Interdependency doesn't only make sense under our own roof. Grandparents can be a part of this supportive relationship as well.

Many grandparents are actively involved in raising their grandchildren. And there are those, like my kids' grandparents, who are separated by distance. Either near or far, grandparents play an important role in their grandkids' lives when they choose to be intentional about connection.

Research at the University of Oxford supports the importance of grandparents in their grandchildren's lives. In a study of 1,500 children, those who were connected and involved with grandparents had fewer behavior and emotional problems.

Scripture mentions the active role Grandma Lois played in her grandson, Timothy's, spiritual development. "I am reminded of your sincere faith, which first lived in your grandmother Lois and in your mother Eunice and, I am persuaded, now lives in you also" (2 Timothy 1:5).

A relationship with a grandparent is impactful. Kids are always listening and watching. They observe and evaluate. Grandchildren want an authentic relationship with their grandparents. The kids desire honesty, commitment, and genuine affection. Their parents hope for encouragement and support from their parents.

Parents are busy people; grandparents are a little less rushed. Like Timothy's grandmother, grandmas and grandpas can choose to establish a strong relationship with their grandchildren.

Intentional interdependent relationships start with a strong bond of love. The grandparent's role is less about protection and provision and more about nurturing, teaching, and guiding.

My father-in-law died before he could be a grandpa. He would have been a really good granddad. He loved kids, had a big ol' belly laugh, and his eyes sparkled with mischief when he was teasing.

Shortly after Kendra, our fourth and youngest child was born, my mother-in-law, Marianne, married Bob. I guess he would be considered my stepfather-in-law.

Bob loved his grandkids, all of them. Step, adopted, birth . . . none of it mattered . . . they were all his and he was proud of his entire family. Papa died a few years ago, but the life lessons he modeled remain. Someday I hope to be a grandparent. If this happens, God willing, I will remember what I learned about being a grandparent from Bob.

> Be intentional. To make extended family time happen, you have to plan it, invest in it, and make an effort.
> Cherish and value your time together. Talk about important things like faith and politics.
> Have fun. Play games.
> Jump into the family mix and pitch in. Don't sit on the sidelines.
> Take time to listen to and be interested in each person. Papa was a master at this.
> Have a sense of humor. Bob and Marianne laughed when Scruffy, our 110 pound Airedale, jumped on their bed in the morning when they were visiting us.

Pass along a skill. Bob taught Jake and Samantha how to make soup.

Tell stories. Grandkids are mesmerized when their Nana and Papa talk about the "olden days."

Be humble. Don't take yourself too seriously.

Remember you are the grandparent and not the child's parent. If discipline is needed and the parents are there, let the parents handle the situation.

Let your grandchildren see you read your Bible and hear you pray.

Tell your grandchildren your faith stories. "We will not hide them from their descendants; we will tell the next generation the praiseworthy deeds of the LORD, his power, and the wonders he has done" (Psalm 78:4).

LONG DISTANCE TRAINING

"I wish we didn't live on opposite coasts," Stacey, my sister-in-law, lamented when we were living in Southern California. The 2,660 miles between San Diego and Baltimore made it more challenging to stay connected.

Most of us hope our kids won't go too far when they go off to college. "I hope my son (or daughter) doesn't fall in love with someone from out of state," is a frequent fear spoken by many moms. We want to keep them close.

Distance doesn't have to mean separation. We can adjust. The Crosby family highly values interdependency. I asked Laura, a master connector, how she and her husband John maintain a close relationship with their young adult daughters despite the miles between them.

"Connection and accessibility are high values in our family. Our two grown daughters live on opposite coasts of the United States, and my husband and I live smack dab in the middle. Not optimal for accessibility and in-person communication, right? But texting and FaceTime to the rescue!

"A practice our daughter, Maggie, instituted is, 'The View from Here.' Every once in a while one of us will initiate a group text with a photo attached, showing the view from our location. It helps us enter into each other's everyday life while we are far apart. We get to see one another's work environment or community.

"The girls and I text each other 24/7. Many crucial decisions are made by text. In fact, we never enter a dressing room without texting each other for outfit consultation."

Flying from Colorado to Maryland, Kendra and I had a conversation with a dad who sat in the aisle seat. We discussed how life changes and the adjustments that must be made as children become young adults.

"When my son left for college, there went my tech support," he shook his head.

"I know! When Kendra left for school there went my fashion consultant." I felt his pain.

After reading Laura's suggestion, I am going to be more millennial-ish and work that phone. Distance doesn't have to be stumbling block to accessibility and connection.

GRAND CONNECTIONS

Susan Mathis, author, mom, and grandma, regularly connects with her grandchildren who live in Cape Town, South Africa.

I asked Susan how she was able to nurture that relationship with an ocean between them.

"In today's world, families are spread all over the globe. It's wonderful I can travel and be with my grandchildren in just a day and a half instead of the several weeks' voyage by ship people used to endure. Rather than seeing them gather around the Sunday dinner table, I can still see my beautiful grandchildren, hear their sweet voices, and watch them grow—through Skype. I learn about their day-to-day activities on Facebook, get photos in emails, enjoy videos over WhatsApp, and I can send gifts by couriers who travel to South Africa.

"We've established a weekly Skype tradition that we all count on and love. Grandpa, who is known to love sweets, has a milk-and-sweetie party with the girls. Our granddaughters fully expect and thoroughly enjoy hearing me read them a story.

"I have to say, the best tradition of all is our blowing-kisses ritual. It started with just a few sweet girlie kisses blown my way and several grandma kisses blown theirs. The kisses have become hurricane kisses that blow me off my chair and baseball kisses that Grandpa catches in his invisible mitt. This loving exchange flies across the pond through cyberspace and lands right in their hearts and ours.

"I admit that sometimes it aches. I hunger for their face-to-face presence, their touch—their hugs and kisses. Yet I take comfort in the fact we have all this wonderful technology at our fingertips. The phone and internet provide multiple ways in which to connect.

"I count my blessings. I am able to connect with my grandbaby Peyton, my three-year-old Devyn, my five-year-old Madison, and my seven-year-old Reagan, either by Skype or in person. Yesterday, I watched ten-month-old Peyton crawl for the first time on a video sent through WhatsApp! In the end, no matter how we make the grandparenting journey happen, there is nothing more wonderful, more joyful, and more fulfilling than hearing my grandkids call me Gran!"

Just as Susan shared, great distance can create heartache. Yet that distance doesn't have to stifle relationships. Families separated by miles just have to get creative. Kirk Weaver, Family Time Training founder, took time to share with me how his friends, an Arizona aunt and uncle, made a positive impact on their Oregon nephew.

"Every month the Ashtons sent their nine-year-old nephew Tim $20 with the following recommendations: Give 10 percent to church or some other ministry, use 10 percent to do something nice for a family member or friend, save 10 percent for your future education. With the remaining 70 percent, buy or save for something you need or want. Over the miles they were training Tim how to save, share, and spend his money wisely.

"Tim would write back and tell the Ashtons how he used the money. Mrs. Ashton showed me two binders filled with letters from Tim. Together we read how he had given money to his church, to feed the hungry, to clothe the poor, and to help build a chapel at his school."

Kirk offers this encouragement to other families who are separated by distance, "With regular contact and an intentional plan, we can develop and strengthen long distance relationships. We can even encourage character development!"

THE SHIFT

Ages and life stages constantly change. Gone are the days when I could confidently say my child is fourteen months old. Now I have to pause and think, is he twenty-six or twenty-seven years old? The different phases do not mean relationships are cut off. They just shift.

Sherri Crandall can relate.

In her blog post "Mothering—A Bittersweet Journey" for 1corinthians13parenting.com, she says, "My house is quiet. It's a new normal for me. I am the mom of four kids, which lends itself to a noisy and sometimes chaotic house. . . . Our daughter is now the only one left at home; her brothers have all taken off to new life chapters. It is a new chapter for those of us left at home too—we are learning our new rhythms.

"I swear it was yesterday when this sweet older lady, probably my current age of fifty, looked at me sympathetically as I was navigating the grocery aisle with two little boys who were punching each other and the two littles in the cart were both crying. She came over and told me how she missed those days and that all her children were now grown and she wished she could trade me a few days. Trust me, I was wishing we actually could. I remember she had tears in her eyes, and her melancholy laced words were so sweet and really encouraged me. She told me to enjoy the years as they were growing up because they go by so quickly. I truly did enjoy them and she was right; they are over in the blink of an eye.

"My emotional musings were prompted by my twenty-one-year-old driving away to pursue his country music career in Nashville and my eighteen-year-old heading off to college. Two really big goodbyes in two short weeks; my heart was not ready. . . .

"I have read at least a dozen blogs over the past few weeks advising me on what to say, what not to say to my adult children. How often you should call your college kids, how you should prepare their siblings, how you should get a new hobby. Some great advice and some I don't recall. In the end we as a family have to figure out our new norm. Like so much of parenting, we don't know what it will be like until we are there. . . .

"I have shed some tears. Like when my husband and I went to dinner with dear friends, and I started crying in the salad bar line or when I was at the grocery store and realized I didn't need to buy all the loaves of bread, gallons of milk, and a dozen apples. Teary as I restocked the shelves and walked away with my new, much smaller basket. Adjusting is part of the life journey.

"I got to my car that day and my cell phone rang. It was my oldest calling to see if he could come over for dinner and asking me how I was doing with his brothers being gone. I gladly walked back into the store and bought things to prepare a bigger dinner. Life is constantly changing, and I accept the challenge, thankful and secure that God is in control of it all."

I can relate to Sherri's story. When I would set the table for dinner a sadness would wash over me for vacant chairs of my college kids. Then the younger ones began having more guests for dinner. I agree that adjusting is part of the journey, but I must admit I still make a lot of food for meals . . . just in case.

THE IN-LAW

When Jake walked into our house with Jaime, I knew this was the woman my son was going to marry. Once they got engaged, congrats and blessings streamed onto social media. Jake's three sisters affirmed the relationship with, "Jaime, you have always been a part of our family," and, "Now I can call you my sister!"

Jake's marriage gives me a new label, mother-in-law. I want to support, love, and encourage my son and his bride. Thankfully I have been in mother-in-law training for over thirty years. I came to this new role prepared.

Without either of us realizing it, Marianne, my mother-in-law, has been training me since Tom and I wed. With grace she has shown me to:

Leave space for the new couple to grow.
Keep priorities straight: The couple first (the marriage) then the extended family.
The relationship is adult to adult. (Not adult to adult-child.)
Foster a relationship with my daughter-in-law that is independent of the one with my son.
When asked, offer suggestions gently.
Pitch in when needed.
Take time for girl-talk and sharing hearts.
Love and delight in the grandkids (when the time comes).
Be available while respecting privacy.
Have fun together.

Marianne sets in-law boundaries for herself. She's the mom of a grown son and appropriately steps back. By doing this she smooths the way for me to step into Tom's family of origin. I know I belong. I hope my relationship with my daughter-in-law will mirror what Marianne has set in motion. I love being with and talking to her. She makes it easy for me to share my heart with her. We laugh together a lot. She has mentored me well. I hope for the verse in Proverbs 31:28 to be a part of my legacy.

Her children arise and call her blessed.

A bird's-eye view gives us a proper perspective when roles shift, loss occurs, or circumstances change. Personal tunnel vision prevents flexibility and halts healthy interconnectedness. Attempting to walk the same direction we always have in spite of big changes only makes the adjustment more difficult or more painful.

Whatever is given up in control (when our roles or circumstances change) can be gained back tenfold in relationship. The sun has set on my highly involved parenting. A new day has begun. My mom role has morphed from a highly involved parent into a supportive one. With every new adjustment, I confidently know God has this too.

There is a time for everything, and a season for every activity under the heavens. —Ecclesiastes 3:1

CHAPTER 11

SUPERNATURAL CONNECTION

Instead, be filled with the Spirit, speaking to one another with psalms, hymns, and songs from the Spirit. Sing and make music from your heart to the Lord, always giving thanks to God the Father for everything, in the name of our Lord Jesus Christ.
—Ephesians 5:18–20

"What is God teaching you this year? What would be your one word?"

My friend Elsa posed these questions to Lindee, Suanne, and me over salads at The Cow restaurant in my quaint little Colorado mountain town of Morrison. At first I couldn't come up with anything. Then God popped the image of thirty-seven pennies into my head.

"*Trust*, that's my word. That's what God is teaching me."

I wrestle with waiting on God. When I wait, my trust begins to waver and fear seeps in. It is so much easier to trust when being still isn't involved in the process.

When I walk Murphy, my rust colored labradoodle with blond highlights (some may say gray fur), I talk with God. I lament, I give thanks, and I petition. Sometimes my mom prayer sounds like this, "Come on, God. No more still small voice. Let's get this going."

I know. That's not very spiritual. But the God of the Universe isn't hurt or offended by my words because He knows my mother's heart.

One Thursday morning, my big dog and I stepped outside for our daily walk. I noticed a penny as we crossed from the concrete driveway to the blacktop street. My son Jake would not have passed it by; he would have picked it up. My friend Pam would have retrieved it and pondered its message, "In God we trust." I thought about the preciousness of that copper coin as Murphy and I made our way down to the path around the lake. I decided I needed to pocket that penny on the return route. God was reminding me to trust Him.

As Murphy and I returned to the edge of the driveway, I bent down to retrieve the penny. I noticed there was a second one about five inches away. I grabbed that one too. Then I saw a few more and picked up each one. Oh my goodness, there were thirty-seven pennies scattered in front of my driveway.

"There must be something significant about the number thirty-seven," I deduced. I got on my computer to see how many times "trust in God" is written about in the Bible. In the NIV it is mentioned thirty-eight times. I bolted out to the driveway, determined to find that thirty-eighth penny. It was nowhere to be found.

For five days I lamented not finding that final penny. On Tuesday morning, I told my prayer partner Vicki about the pennies and the missing thirty-eighth.

"Do you know what my favorite Psalm is?"

"No." I probably should know, we have prayed together every Tuesday for eight years. "It's Psalm 37. Look it up."

I did. Psalm 37 is all about trusting God in the struggle. Those words were heaven sent.

That psalm contained the message I needed. I would have felt satisfied finding the thirty-eighth penny but I would have missed out on the psalmist's words.

Recently I searched "trust in God" again on Biblegateway.com for the New International Version (NIV). It now displays thirty-seven results, go figure. Our God is a God of miracles.

PRICELESS PRAYER

God has moved me to look at prayer through heaven's eyes. If my kids only came to me with requests (demands dressed up nicely), of course I would be glad to hear them. I love being with my kids, listening to them, and hearing their heart's desires. When my children come to me with a grateful heart—expressing appreciation, I feel blessed and honored.

Those types of exchanges are priceless. If their tender thoughts are penned, I save the notes and cards.

Families face different challenges and victories throughout life. We are not alone in our struggles or in our successes; we have each other and we have a great God. Our family's interdependence and a God dependence are sources of support and encouragement.

When your family faces a difficulty like unemployment, health issues, or tragedy or when your little gang experiences a great joy such as new baby, better job, and good family time, let your kids see you talking to God, trusting Him, and praising Him.

If you have not yet done this, don't be discouraged. You can start today. We serve a God who is omnipresent, omnipotent, and omniscient. He created time and is not bound by it like we are. He can move in and through it as He pleases to accomplish His will. He can make time up in the air!

God winks and God-incidences, like my thirty-seven pennies story, are moments to share with your kids. Our kids love to hear God stories. Both our personal stories and the ones penned in Scripture.

Janet Thompson is the author of *Forsaken God? Remembering the Goodness of God Our Culture Has Forgotten*. In her blog post, "Passing on Family Stories through the Generations" on my blog, she says, "Telling family stories of God's goodness keeps the memories alive. We all have them; we need to share them with our children and grandchildren."

Janet adds, "It's our job to ensure that God's unchanging Word prevails and reigns through future generations. We need to pass on the hope we have in Christ by equipping the next generation to read and understand the Bible and accept Jesus as their personal Savior— not encumber them with rules easily broken, but guide them toward a relationship they wouldn't forfeit or jeopardize for anything or anyone."

A DANGEROUS QUESTION

Christians are not immune to bad things. Some young people feel God can't be trusted because He allows bad things to happen.

Fall semester of my freshman year in college, I took a philosophy course called Ethics in Society. I may have been the only Christian in the class. My professor was hungry for a debate. I was the meal. He posed the question, "If there is a God, a God who is love, why does He allow bad things to happen?"

I was unprepared for that argument. I had a faith without teeth or reason. I left that hour feeling beat up. Even worse, I felt as though I failed God. I was unable to articulate or defend my beliefs.

Author Tim Shoemaker says in his blog post, "1 Question You Must Answer Before Your Kids Leave for College," for 1corinthians13 parenting.com, "[How can a loving God allow bad things to happen to good people] is the question parents haven't fully prepared their kids to answer—and the enemy knows it. The enemy has used this question on kids away at college to effectively weaken their faith—or worse. . . . 'How can a loving God allow bad things to happen to good people?' sounds almost harmless on the surface. You've asked the same question yourself. But this is an iceberg question. The real danger lies deeper. Unless you help your kids find answers to this question they're vulnerable. They're in danger. Because if your kids doubt God's love, every other part of their faith will take a hit. God's love is foundational to everything we believe, right? 'For God so loved the world.'

"Here's a crash course on three basic reasons God allows bad things to happen to 'good' people.

1. "We live in a fallen world. Bad things happen to nice and nasty people. Man chose sin back in the Garden of Eden and has lived with the consequences ever since. Someday God will change all that but until He does bad things will continue to happen—to everyone.
2. "Bad things keep us on the right tracks. When everything is rosy, people tend to drift from God. It's a sad fact of life. Sometimes

God allows bad things to happen to nudge us closer to him—and to keep us from really getting ourselves in trouble.

3. "Bad things make us shine for Christ like we never could before. Sometimes bad things change us—for the better—in ways we can't imagine.

"Sometimes God allows the natural consequences of poor choices to bend us, break us, and shake up our world. Then something changes inside our heart. It is only then that Christ can shine through us like He never could before. Maybe we mess up somehow. Or get extremely embarrassed. Or lose our job. Or maybe we don't get accepted by the school or program we applied for. We feel crushed. But as God helps us through our bending and breaking experiences, we will later be able to help others through theirs. And likely we'll be a lot more compassionate and sensitive to them. And we'll understand them like we wouldn't have before. . . .

"Even if your kids are going to a Christian college, they need to understand why God allows bad things to happen to 'good' people. Remember, simply going to a Christian college doesn't necessarily make your kids safer. Our enemy doesn't avoid Christian colleges. He infiltrates. There will be intelligent students and winsome professors who are good at getting kids to question their faith."

Whether a child is homeschooled, attends a private school, or a public school Tim's three reasons why bad things happen to nice people will be helpful when encountering other world views as mentioned in Colossians 2:8:

> See to it that no one takes you captive through hollow and deceptive philosophy.

WHY BELIEVE?
College professors are not the only ones who ask good questions. Kids do too. In his blog post for 1corinthians13parenting.com, "A Missile in a Minivan," Jim Dempsey tells about his experience with his teen daughter.

"From the back seat of the minivan, the missile was launched, 'Daddy, why do you believe in Jesus, Christianity, you know, all that stuff?'

"Everyone in the family was asleep but my youngest daughter and me. We were driving home from a visit to my in-laws.

"With a quick prayer, here's how I answered my young teen:

1. "I believe the evidence for a Creator is clear. The creation is too complex and living beings too complicated to be explained by evolution.

2. "If a Creator made the world out of nothing, then there is no other miracle that would be too difficult for that Creator. Thus, the Bible's miracles are possible.

3. "If this Creator made me reasoning and curious, I believe He made me want to know about Him. Thus, we should have stories of His dealings with men down through the ages.

4. "Of all the stories (religions), only Christianity explains the world I see. I see horrible sin, so I know that sin exists. I see sin in myself, so I know that I am sinful. I see an amazing earth that spins just the right distance from the sun to make liquid water possible, and an atmosphere of just the right mixture to sustain life. Hundreds of other facts prove our Creator is good. But my sin has separated me from Him. I need a way to be reconciled to Him.

5. "The way of reconciliation is credibly supplied in Jesus. Because miracles are possible, I am willing to read the New Testament accounts of Jesus and consider them credible. Since the writers of the Gospels do not make themselves out to be superheroes, these writings ring true. Since the followers of Jesus claimed He rose from the grave, and were willing to die horrible deaths rather than recant, I believe they reported exactly what they saw.

6. "The New Testament books were written soon after Jesus' Resurrection and jealously guarded. They were written in Greek, a common language, and there is no controversy today over

what the words mean. Many copies of these books survive today, so anyone can compare and determine if any changes had been made. The New Testament is both reliable and inspired.

7. "If Jesus is God and the New Testament is inspired, then whatever Jesus commands, I must do. I still sin, but I believe that the infinite value of Christ's death paid for my sin.

8. "Jesus spoke of hell so I believe in it.

9. "Since I believe in hell, I take my parenting duties seriously.

"Just because you have one conversation with your child, don't think the matter is closed. Keep the spiritual dialogue going. And teenagers have a keen eye for hypocrisy. Show your child your behavior matches your core beliefs."

Jim was prepared with his nine points. He was able to articulate his beliefs in a clear way to his daughter. I have always had faith. God has used hard times and miraculous moments to grow and deepen it. Like me, if you have always believed in God and never really questioned His existence, it may be difficult to communicate why you believe what you believe to your kids. Jim takes us through a logical and easy to follow progression: creation, sin, reconciliation, then to eternity. It is critical we can handle those unexpected missiles launched by our kids at unpredictable times. As it says in 1 Peter 3:15, we need to be ready.

> But sanctify Christ as Lord in your hearts, always being
> ready to make a defense to everyone who asks you to
> give an account for the hope that is in you, yet with
> gentleness and reverence.

DISTRACTIONS THAT HINDER

"He's annoring me," our then almost three-year-old daughter Kendra would say when her older brother Jake was bothering her. She merged the words annoying and ignoring to create the word annoring.

When a person ignores us it is annoying. When we are annoyed sometimes we ignore the annoyer. But what if instead we taught our kids that annoyances can be a catalyst for prayer?

We endured a tough six month season in our family. Our daughter Courtney went AWOL. She had moved out and moved in with her significant other. We didn't know where she was living for a portion of that time. Thankfully, God swooped in and supernaturally intervened. Suffice it to say we had a huge victory. Courtney had reached out and called me. She disclosed where she was living. This was a real God-boasting kind of win. I was overjoyed and wanted to do the King David happy dance—though fully clothed of course (2 Samuel 6:14).

Only a couple of hours later I received an unkind blow. My happy feet were knocked out from under me. So often after a spiritual victory comes an attack. I wasn't ready. I was shocked. Instead of rejoicing, the incident annoyed and distracted me. It occupied way too much space in my brain.

The unkind act was getting in the way of my joy. My thoughts were bouncing from *how mean* to *this person must be really hurting to do this*. The volley of thoughts whipped back and forth from self-righteous anger to compassion.

After a short time of playing mental ping-pong, my friend Nina gave me a call. (Don't you love it when God moves a friend to call just at the very right time?) I filled her in, and she advised, "Don't let this steal your joy. Every time you think of this situation, pray a prayer of thankfulness about the victory instead."

This was the solution. The unkindness had hindered my parental thankfulness prayers and replaced my joy. So why not use the annoyance as a catalyst for prayer? I must have been highly agitated because I found myself praying a ton. That battle went on throughout the day. Because I was praying so much, I learned something about myself. When I am hurt, I tend to wallow in it. And my pity party would result in me missing critical lessons from the Lord.

When curt comments or toxic verbal weapons are tossed my way I have heard this advice, "Consider the source." But I don't like that. It feels dismissive and sounds like a put down. I know I'm no better than the source. Instead, while processing nastiness, I will choose to remember how people treat others is a reflection of how they feel about themselves or an indication of how they have been treated by someone else. When I look at unkind words or actions in this way, feelings of compassion are generated rather than a big bad mad. Even though unkindness is often delivered as a direct personal hit, I am learning to not take it personally but instead move along and look at what God wants me to concentrate on, learn, or pray about.

AUTHENTICITY OR HYPOCRISY

People we know well can hurt us if we allow them the power to do so. Even people we don't know, like those with whom we share the road, can affect us as well. My friend Mary Heathman shares her experience.

"I pulled up behind a white SUV. The bumper sticker facing me said, 'Honk if you love Jesus.' I complied. As the light remained a steady red the driver jumped out of his car, making grand angry gestures with his arms yelling, 'What's wrong with you? Why are you honking at me?' I chose not to get out of the car. From the safety of my locked door, pointed to the back of his car. He walked between our cars to see what caused me to honk. Sheepishly, he looked down, then at me, and nodded his head."

The irony of the moment wasn't lost on either driver. I like Mary's story because it reminds me of the struggle between the flesh and the spirit.

Being real is really convicting. My faith and my feelings fight for first place in my heart and my mind. I wonder, "Am I a real or cultural Christian? Do I live the belief I profess to hold?"

I confess I am a hypocrite and a Christian. My hypocrisy is not lost on my children when I tell them not to do things I have done. I give advice to others that I don't take myself. I know the best and right way to honor God with my words and my actions and I do the opposite.

I am selfish, prideful, and human. I am a sinner who needs a savior. I am in good company too because—unless your name is Jesus—you too are the worst of all sinners, just like Paul and me (1 Timothy 1:15–16).

We (you, our kids, and I) justify our choices, actions, and behavior.

We normalize. "Everyone sins."

We downsize. "It's not that big of a deal."

We minimize. "It doesn't hurt anyone."

We trivialize. "It's just a little sin."

We strategize. "If no one knows . . ."

We personalize. "It's my life."

We hypothesize. "If he hadn't, then I wouldn't have."

We criticize. "He did that wrong."

We generalize. "Everyone does it."

We overemphasize. "It feels right."

We glamorize. "I'm cool if I [fill in the blank]."

We legitimatize. "It's OK because so many people say it is."

We polarize. "If you don't agree you are against me."

Grace and truth are forgotten. We focus on people pleasing and justification rather than God-glorification.

What is my measuring stick? My feelings? My perception? The culture? Other people's behavior or beliefs? Is Jesus and His Father's never changing and always living Word my plumb line?

The WWJD (What Would Jesus Do) movement of the late 1990s was an attempt to encourage Christians to act like Christ would act, to not be a hypocrite, to not be a cultural Christian.

To act like Jesus is a good start. God pushes the envelope and moves believers to be more like Jesus and less like ourselves. We are saved sinners who want to honor and glorify God, to synthesize our faith with our life. The solution to the sinner struggle is confession, surrender, and repentance.

How do we help our kiddos hear God's voice and know His will? We talk the talk, walk the walk, and talk about the walk. We teach, model, and share our faith with our children and grandkids. We read God's Word, pray, and join a community of believers. And in those moments when we act like a hypocrite, we dust ourselves off and get back up again on a path pleasing to God. When we are transparent about our struggles with faith and living in the tension of grace and truth in a sinful world, our kids' eyes are opened to see the person of Jesus and a relationship with Him as a real one—one to grow and chase after. I don't want to be a hypocrite but just to be safe, I've made a conscious decision not to put a fish on the back of my car.

THE COLLISON OF FEAR AND FAITH

Tom and I attended church one Saturday evening. The sermon series was based on 1 Corinthians 11, a timely message for a culture debating sexual identity and bathroom choices. A good portion of the sermon was on gender roles and appearance. My oldest daughter, a young adult, has gender identity confusion. She planned to attend church on Sunday the following day.

Do I want my daughter to embrace her femininity, to feel comfortable in her womanhood? Yes, of course. Do I want my kid to get hurt? No, of course not.

We bounced back and forth, "Should we warn her?"

Fear was crowding out trust. *What if she never comes back to church?*

I thought back to my pennies on the sidewalk. Can I trust God thirty-seven cents worth?

Tom and I decided to let faith win over fear. I struggled mightily over this. It went against my mama bear instincts to protect her. I had to recall God's great love for my child (bigger than mine) and God's knowledge of her (deeper than mine). I needed to remember who my God is: faithful, good, all knowing, ever present, all powerful. I cried a big ugly cry.

Sunday night Tom asked Courtney how she felt during the sermon.

"To be honest, it was really hard." Tears filled her eyes. My mom heart ached for her.

"I'm so proud of you for staying and listening. You are so brave. Why didn't you get up and walk out?"

"Nick was preaching from the Bible. He wasn't stating his opinion, just God's Word. He said his message in love."

Courtney received both truth and love. God taught me trust and faith. The Lord is working on both of us. When I struggle with trust, I ask myself, "Can I trust God thirty-seven cents worth?"

Psalm 37:3–7 reminds me to trust God while I wait for Him to move.

> *Trust in the LORD and do good; dwell in the land and enjoy safe pasture. Take delight in the LORD, and he will give you the desires of your heart. Commit your way to the LORD; trust in him and he will do this: He will make your righteous reward shine like the dawn, your vindication like the noonday sun. Be still before the LORD and wait patiently for him.*

GET OUT OF THE WAY

Protecting my kids from pain is a parental instinct. Not protecting our kids from conviction isn't compassionate; it is enabling. In the spirit of interdependence and God dependence, we can and sometimes must move out of the way and allow the natural consequences to take place. God can use this type of correction for good. Then we can come alongside our child and help clean up the mess. With a humble "everybody spills" attitude of we can reach down, pull our child up, and help clean up.

This goes against our parent protective grain. It takes prayer and determination to submit to God's will and way.

There are times God uses natural consequences to get our attention, face our sin, and help us see things more clearly. It isn't pretty, but it is effective. In *Out of a Far Country*, Christopher Yuan tells how God used jail time to change him, restore his relationship with his parents, and commit his life to Christ. The natural consequence of sinful living was what God used to redeem Christopher.

I imagine Christopher's parents experienced great heartache when he was in jail. Sadly, sometimes the natural consequences fallout can be harsh: jail, expulsion from school, detention, or removal from a team, yet it might actually be God's mercy and protection. If Christopher hadn't landed in jail he may have never experienced God's grace and relationship restoration with his parents. God can use difficult things and consequences for our actions to draw us closer to Him.

Listen to the humility of the Psalmist in 119:66–68, "Teach me knowledge and good judgment, for I trust your commands. Before I was afflicted I went astray, but now I obey your word. You are good, and what you do is good; teach me your decrees."

The psalmist recognizes God's ways, even His correction, are good.

JESUS LOVES YOU

It is not enough just to tell our kids Jesus loves them. We need to sincerely act on and verbalize our convictions and faith. We must be honest about what we know or don't know. Integrate faith into everyday life and conversations. Be quick to forgive and take responsibility for your own sinfulness and show remorse and repentance. Demonstrate how to repair and reconcile relationships. Layering is the answer.

No matter what choices my kids make, they don't even need to ask what Tom and I think about something because we have been careful to express our belief system and act on our principles. This is not an easy road. Especially as children become young adults and make some pretty big life decisions that have just as large consequences. (If you find yourself in this nasty position—keep loving your kids while being true to who you are. And for the record, I'm sorry. This can be very painful; I intimately know this heartache.)

Even though young adults are interested in a mother and father's point of view, they sometimes (often) choose to act independent of it. At the end of the day the parent's opinion or anyone else's really doesn't matter. Only one opinion does, our Heavenly Father's.

Misty Honnold, a single mom of four and founder of a single mom ministry, tells us how to train our kids to hear God's voice in her article for 1corinthians13parenting.com, "Single Mothers Raising Future Fathers."

"When my boys would take a seemingly wrong turn, I would calm my heart by remembering who God is and His promise over them. For each of my children I have individual scriptural promises I believe God has given me that I speak over them. When I write to them, I jot down a part of the verse. When they are in trouble, I remind them of God's promise over their lives. His Word is alive, and we can use it.

"Help your sons learn the Father's voice. This is by far the greatest way we can help our sons succeed as fathers, but it means work for us. It means we have to know the voice and leadership of the Father. It means we have to display before our sons what it means to hear His voice and follow His voice. We can learn who the Father is, how He leads, and His character in the Word. So we have to be in the Word to lead our sons to that place of knowing His voice."

God is with us. I pray my children will hear His voice, see His hand, seek His face, and read His Word. "Lord, draw my children to Yourself. Please give them a heart, mind, body, and soul that depends on You. Amen."

Pray mountain-moving prayers on your children's behalf. Matthew 17:20 reminds us of the power of prayer.

> He replied, "Because you have so little faith. Truly I tell you, if you have faith as small as a mustard seed, you can say to this mountain, 'Move from here to there,' and it will move. Nothing will be impossible for you."

Conclusion

THE DECLARATION OF INTERDEPENDENCE

As the Father has loved me, so have I loved you. Now remain in my love. —John 15:9

Tom and I went to Taiwan to visit our daughter Samantha while she was there teaching English. During our trip, she arranged for the three of us to take a small plane over to Orchid (also called Lanyu) Island about fifty miles off the coast. We rented two scooters, with me as the consummate rider, and toured the twenty-nine square miles of the small island. As we were exploring we noticed fifteen or so scooters parked at what appeared to be an overlook. We decided to check it out. We climbed some wooden steps until there were no more. We continued on a skinny dirt path up the hill. The people descending were covered in mud. They handed us their walking sticks and enthusiastically exclaimed, "You can do it!"

Do what? I thought we were just going to a scenic overlook. Our climb became increasingly more challenging. It included grabbing vines to ascend farther and holding on to tall weeds to avoid falling due to the slippery mud. The final destination turned out to be beautiful Heaven Lake, a volcanic crater.

A few days following the hike we were speaking with some Taiwanese friends. "Oh, we would never go on the hike to Heaven Lake. There are too many poisonous snakes and spiders."

Poisonous snakes and giant wood spiders call Orchid Island home.

THE WEB

Giant wood spiders range in length from five to seven inches. The webs they spin are enormous. Have you ever examined a spider web? Beauty, strength, and purpose are all components of a web.

A typical United States spiderweb takes a beating from a trapped fly but it won't fail. It is strong and stretchy. When a piece of the web is pulled, it only fails in that spot. The spider repairs its web rather than replacing it.

If we weave family relationships like a web they will be strong and stretchy. They will be able to withstand adversity and recover from it. The components of peace making, appreciating unique qualities, acknowledging imperfection, being honest, having a sense of humor, and a willingness to be open are six strands looped together to create a healthy interdependent environment. When family relationships are strong and stretchy, robust and flexible, resilient and pliable, they will be interdependent relationships that last a lifetime.

We were not prepared for our hike to Heaven Lake. We weren't wearing the right shoes or clothes, we didn't bring water bottles, and we were uninformed about the dangers along the way. Nevertheless we continued to hike. That's sort of OK for an adventure but not a good approach to family life. So often we step forward day after day without being intentional in connection or the messages we give our kiddos. We know how to troubleshoot for the moment but forget to plan for the long haul.

Humans are created for connection. God designed families for this purpose. He also wants to be known by His creation. He shows Himself in nature, His Word, and by sending His Son. He beckons us to come to Him, abide in Him, and depend on Him.

God has placed within each of us a need to be in community and in a relationship with the Lord. We want to know that we matter to others and to God. We ask, "Mom, Dad, do you see me? Really see me?" "Do you know me, God? Do I matter? Does my life have purpose?"

The God who sees says yes to these questions. We matter because He created us on purpose for a purpose.

How would our kiddos say we, their parents, would answer these questions? Do we really see and know our children? Have we communicated they are important to us, the family, and to others? Do we assure them their life has meaning and purpose?

The affirmative answer to these questions is found in connection, interdependence. Independence does not satisfy the human longing for belonging and purpose. If the goal for our children is independence, over time they will become increasingly emotionally distant and seek out other more connected and satisfying relationships.

The Declaration of Interdependence

In my family we will:
> Be respectful.
> Be responsible for ourselves, our words, and our actions.
> Demonstrate kindness.
> Encourage each other.
> Give space for grace.
> Speak truth.
> Show mercy.
> Seek justice.
> Apply self-control.
> Find solutions to problems.
> Support one another.
> Speak love loud.
> Help each other.
> Dialogue not debate.
> Converse not coerce.
> Listen rather than lecture.
> Ask instead of assume.
> Pray for one another.
> Pray with each other.
> Seek God.
> Honor the Lord with our words, thoughts, and deeds.
> Be present.
> Show gratitude.
> Have fun.
> Laugh together.
> Cry together.

Withstand adversity.

Play.

Hug.

Forgive.

Ask for forgiveness.

Be OK when life spills occur.

Allow for human mistakes because everyone spills.

Help each other out in the messes.

Build connections that last a lifetime.

CATS AND DOGS

Over Christmas break a few years ago, Tom and I took our four college kids to Islamorada in the Florida Keys. We drove across the Seven Mile Bridge to explore the Everglades. One of the spots we visited was the Everglades Alligator Farm. The best part of the farm wasn't seeing the alligators or even taking the airboat ride (which got stuck and we all had to get out—into the swampy water where the gators and snakes reside—and push the boat out.) The highlight was watching a black lab and a Florida Panther.

A large sign hung on the cage, "If separated, will stress-out." The two unlikely pals played chase, wrestled, and cuddled. We were captivated watching this unusual pair interact.

The lab and the panther remind me of my four kids and how they complement one another. Their talents and interests are diverse but they still enjoy being together and appreciate each other.

Over the years God has impressed upon me to be a relationship builder not a relationship buster. Family dynamics are complicated and not always harmonious.

Our parenting journey can get messy. If it isn't already, at some point it most likely will. A family that is interdependent and God dependent will have more success navigating life when the unexpected comes.

When life spills happen, we need each other. Independence will not satisfy that innate desire we have for relationship. We want to know it is OK because everybody spills. Connected families are confident in the knowledge that we can lean on our loved ones as they walk alongside us. We are able to depend on our great big God because He is always with us. He prepares the way before us, comes alongside us, and is our rear guard.

We are created for connection. Not just while our kids reside under our roof but for a lifetime and an eternity. The interdependence string isn't so tight that it breaks or chokes its contents, nor too loose so the individual pieces fall out. Just the right tension of tautness and slack is needed. Interdependent families are bound together with heartstrings. Independent families hang together in the good times and hard times.

When the spills in life come, we know it is OK; everyone spills, and our family will be with us to help clean up the mess.

> *Bear with each other and forgive one another if any of you has a grievance against someone. Forgive as the Lord forgave you. And over all these virtues put on love, which binds them all together in perfect unity.*
> *—Colossians 3:13–14*

Appendix

101 AFFIRMATIONS TO BLESS YOUR CHILD'S HEART[1]

You may need help verbalizing affirmation if your native love language is quality time, receiving gifts, acts of service, or physical touch. Here are three guidelines to keep in mind when articulating affirmation: Speak truthfully. Speak sincerely. Speak specifically.

We all need affirmation. Some need it more than others. These messages can be delivered verbally, in written form, or via text.

I like you

I love you.

I like the person you are becoming.

I love spending time with you. Would you like to come with me when I [fill in the blank]?

I am so thankful God gave you to me!

I have noticed you are a good decision maker. You really thought [fill in the blank] through.

If I were your age, we would be friends for sure!

I appreciate your willingness to [fill in the blank].

I love your sense of humor.

I thought about you when I saw [fill in the blank].

I wish you were with me when [fill in the blank].

I missed you today when [fill in the blank].

I know God has great plans for you!

I appreciate the way you help me [fill in the blank].

I have confidence in your ability to figure this out.

---

[1]Lori Wildenberg, "101 Was to Bless Your Child's Heart," accessed May 24, 2018, https://loriwildenberg.com/2015/08/24/101-ways-to-bless-your -childs-heart/.

I appreciate your respectful attitude.

I can count on you.

I told [grandparent, friend, etc.] I am proud of you.

I noticed how you asked [friend, sibling, etc.] about his/her day. I am certain that made him/her feel good.

I love hearing about your day.

I look forward to seeing you walk through the door.

I love watching you and [sibling, friend] spend time together.

I see Jesus in you.

My heart sings when you hug me.

The best part of my day is spending time with you.

It makes me feel happy when you are with me.

This project is quality work. I am sure it feels good to give your best effort.

Thank you for [fill in the blank].

Thank you for doing [fill in the blank]. You are responsible.

Thank you for helping me with [fill in the blank]. You are considerate.

Listening to you sing makes me so happy.

You make me smile.

You made God smile when you [fill in the blank] today.

You give the best hugs.

You are so brave. I noticed how you [fill in the blank].

You have a lot of patience. You really took your time with [fill in the blank].

You are so thoughtful. Thanks for remembering [fill in the blank].

Your laugh is contagious.

You make me laugh.

You are amazing. When I was your age I would never have been able to [fill in the blank].

You have a big heart.

You have a gentle soul.

You are special.

You are important.

Your life impacts others.

You did this all on your own. Wow! Impressive.

You are a blessing to me and your [mom/dad, friend, teacher, etc.].

You are so smart. How did you come up with that?

You really hung in there when the going got tough. You know how to persevere.

You are honest. Honesty is usually not convenient and often costs something. But it is always worth it.

You are truthful and kind. What a great combination.

You are patient. You demonstrated patience when you [fill in the blank].

You showed humility. You made [fill in the blank] feel special.

You are courageous. You exhibited courage when you [fill in the blank].

You are generous.

You are content.

You are organized.

You are a good friend.

You showed compassion when [fill in the blank].

You have a good mind. You used it well when [fill in the blank].

You showed respect for authority when [fill in the blank].

You have leadership skills. You know your own mind.

Thanks for suggesting [fill in the blank]. It was a great idea.

Your good manners make being with you a joy.

Even when it's hard, you are respectful.

You managed your frustration well when you [fill in the blank].

You exercised self-control when you [fill in the blank].

You are so gentle with [pet, younger sibling, etc.].

You were unselfish when you [fill in the blank].

You are valuable (Luke 12:24).

You are loved.

You are a fellow citizen with the saints (Ephesian 2:19).
You can move mountains (Mark 11:22–23).
God created you for a special purpose.
God has gifted you with the talent of [fill in the blank].
God has equipped you to [fill in the blank].
When you stood up for what was right, God was cheering you on!
You showed maturity when you [fill in the blank].
You are a child of the King!
You are diligent.
You have a great sense of humor.
It's so great you don't take things too seriously.
Your [brother, sister, grandparent, etc.] thinks you are special.
You are a good listener.
You are capable.
You are lovable.
You are God's gift to Christ (John 17:24).
You are cherished (Ephesian 2:4).
God chose you (1 Peter 2:9).
God says you were created in Christ for good works (Ephesian 2:10).
God delights in you (Zephaniah 3:17).
God sings over you (Zephaniah 3:17).
God is with you (Zephaniah 3:17).
God rejoices over you (Zephaniah 3:17).
God will guard you (2 Timothy 1:12).
God will guide you (Psalm 48:14).
God will help you (Isaiah 44:2).
God equips you (2 Timothy 3:16–17).
God created you in His image (Genesis 1:27).
God will never leave you (Hebrews 13:5).
God loves you (John 3:16).

Affirmations are declarations of the truth. They may be related to a relationship, a skill set, an observable character trait, or a promise of God. Kids need affirmation and encouragement from their parents.

EMOTIONAL SAFETY EVALUATION[2]

Life is full of unexpected ups and downs. Our kids must learn how to be resilient in the midst of disappointments. But they cannot be resilient unless they feel emotionally safe.

If we desire resilient kids, it is up to moms and dads to provide an emotionally safe environment for our kids to experience failure or struggle.

To do this we start by examining ourselves:

Am I trustworthy with confidential information?

Am I sensitive to personal struggles and hopes shared?

Do I refrain from using personal information as a weapon later?

Am I able to handle the small irritations and inconveniences in life with calm and patience?

Am I able to remain calm when bad decisions are made or accidents occur?

Do I avoid comparing my child to his siblings or peers?

Am I able to deal directly with a problem rather than use a passive aggressive approach?

Can I be kind even when I disagree?

Am I real with my kids, letting them know I experience struggles and make mistakes?

Is my home a place where it is OK to be imperfect and a little weird sometimes?

After some honest self-examination and making the necessary adjustments, we are better able to provide an emotionally safe atmosphere for our kids.

---

[2]Lori Wildenberg, "10 Questions to Evaluate Emotional Safety in Your Home," accessed May 24, 2018, https://loriwildenberg.com/2017/07/10/10 -questions-to-evaluate-emotional-safety-in-your-home-eq-part-5/.

EMOTIONAL INTELLIGENCE ASSESSMENT[3]

Do you have a child or young adult who "word vomits" his feelings? After spewing his emotions, he feels better, but you are still in the stench of that emotional expulsion.

How can we train our kids to express their feelings without doing an affect purge? By training them how to recognize and verbalize emotion.

Before putting words to feelings, create awareness and identify triggers. Then our kids will be more able to self-regulate and enjoy more positive relationships with family members and others.

Does your child become defensive when corrected? (correction not criticism)

Is your child able to utilize both positive and negative feedback in a constructive way?

How does your child respond to stressful situations? (lots of homework, a busy schedule)

How does your child respond to disappointment?

Is your child able to persevere and persist in order to meet a goal?

How would you describe your child's general disposition? (optimistic, pessimistic, or realistic)

Is your child's self-talk harmful or helpful?

Is your child able to state his or her concerns constructively?

Is your child able to dialogue and discuss without debating or becoming defensive?

Is your child able to see things from another point of view?

How well does your child play and work with others?

Does your child express empathy for others?

Can your child admit to making a mistake?

---

[3]Lori Wildenberg, "20 Questions to Assess Your Child's Emotional Quotient," accessed May 24, 2018, https://loriwildenberg.com/2017/05/22/20-questions -to-assess-your-childs-emotional-quotient-eq-part-1/.

Is your child able to ask for forgiveness? Grant forgiveness?

Does your child follow through with promises?

Is your child able to be flexible?

Does your child demonstrate respect for others, for God, for self, for property?

Is your child loyal to family members? Friends?

Is your child willing and able to problem-solve?

Does your child seek help when needed?

You may even consider taking the assessment yourself. How we parents respond makes a big impact on our children.

My son, do not let wisdom and understanding out of your sight, preserve sound judgment and discretion; they will be life for you, an ornament to grace your neck. —Proverbs 3:21–22

SOFT SKILLS EVALUATION[4]

We can no longer solely rely on our kids' powers of observation and abilities to interpret interpersonal interaction. Soft skills such as communication, respect, integrity, positive attitude, work ethic, conflict resolution, empathy, time management, and teamwork need to be intentionally taught in the home.

Here are some questions to evaluate your kid's soft skills:

> Is your child able to share?
> Can your child play by the rules?
> Is your child respectful of other people?
> Is your child responsible for his personal stuff?
> Does your child admit when he is wrong and say he is sorry?
> Can your child look others in the eye when speaking or listening?
> Does your child greet people as they enter a room?
> What is your child's general disposition?
> Is your child able to persevere?
> How does your child handle disagreement?

People skills and emotional intelligence are closely linked. EI can be increased and social skills can be taught.

---

[4]Lori Wildenberg, "10 Questions to Assess Your Child's People Skills," accessed May 24, 2018, https://loriwildenberg.com/2017/07/24/10-questions -to-assess-your-childs-people-skills/.

40 GREAT WAYS TO CONNECT

Contributions from The MOMS Together Facebook Group:

Ask, "How can I pray for you?"

Play a Would You Rather question game.

Binge watch a favorite show.

Play board or card games.

Plan a day with your son or daughter doing activities of their choosing.

Build with Lincoln Logs or LEGOs.

Cook and bake.

Do crafts.

Do random acts of kindness anonymously.

Dance.

Take your child, one at a time, on a date night.

Eat together.

Engage in sporting activities.

Find multiple player game apps.

Fish.

Give a shoulder or back massage.

Get a manicure or pedicure with your daughter.

Go to the library.

Have a nighttime chat.

Take a hike or walk.

Indulge in ice cream.

Sing karaoke.

Learn something together.

Let your child teach you something.

Make candies and cookies for friends and neighbors.

Pick apples.

Play I Spy in the car.

Play family trivia.

Play with playdough.
Read aloud.
Play with sidewalk chalk.
Share favorite worship songs.
Shop 'til you drop.
Sing.
Snuggle.
Stay up late.
Take pictures together.
Play the Alphabet Game during long car rides.
Toss the football. Shoot hoops.
Watch a movie together.

These are great ideas on different ways to meet our kids where they are. Consider their interests and personalities when choosing an activity. The activity is the vehicle that facilitates a deeper and stronger connection. These types of interactions help us to be students of our kids so we know their likes, dislikes, fears, hopes, and dreams. We want to be the parents our kids need.

Thank you to Jamie Bates, Lisa Brown, Lisa Edwards Cyr, Sandi Haustein, Cathy Horning, Kristi Kohn, Lisa Leshaw, Jenn Neff, Michelle Nietert, Janice Powell, Christen Price, Heather Riggleman, Rachel Robins, Melanie Shauger, Shannon Shea, Elizabeth Spencer, and Linda Tang.

12 DATING RED FLAGS TO SHARE WITH YOUR SON[5]

Parents are typically better at having dating conversations with the girls. We seem to communicate red flags to our daughters more than to our sons.

Boys are often a little less aware of dating warning signs than girls. Perhaps this is because our sons are more concerned with making a good impression than discerning behavior.

Consider the following types of potential girlfriend qualities that serve as a red flag.

The Damsel in Distress: She can be appealing to a guy for sure. You may find it appealing to save, fix, and be the hero, but this gal plays the victim and doesn't take responsibility for her own behavior.

Drama Queen: Her reactions are outrageous, over the top, and explosive.

The Princess: She needs to be constantly pampered, paid attention to, lavished with gifts, must have designer everything, and treats service people with disdain.

The Jumper: She bounces from one friendship or interest to the next.

The Patient: She is chronically ill (not really ill but pretends to be in order to manipulate another, justify behavior, or to get attention); something is physically wrong *all the time!*

The Debater: She needs to argue constantly. There are more negative conversations than positive ones with her.

Needy Nellie: She is in love with love, not with you. She needs constant contact, validation, and attention. She may even be jealous of your guy friends.

---

[5]Lori Wildenberg, "12 Dating Red Flags to Share with Your Son," accessed May 24, 2018, https://loriwildenberg.com/2016/04/04/12-dating-red-flags-to-share-with-your-son/.

The Rebounder: If she just got out of a relationship, she may not be ready for another.

The Bad Friend: She chooses friends you don't like. Birds of a feather really do flock together.

The Shamer: She disrespects and embarrasses you both publicly and privately.

The Hater: She treats her parents and others (like those in the service industry) with contempt.

The Aggressor: She relentlessly chases down young men and uses her body to manipulate and get attention.

One more: If your family and friends don't like your new girlfriend, investigate this further. These are the folks who have your best interest at heart.

Some of these qualities could be isolated incidents, but if you see a pattern with any of these, heads up and head out!

Let's pray for our boys that they will be wise in their relationships. We are raising our sons to be men, husbands, and dads. And let's train our girls not to be one of these chicks!

> *Charm is deceptive, and beauty is fleeting; but a woman who fears the LORD is to be praised.*
> *—Proverbs 31:30*

12 DATING WARNING SIGNS TO SHARE WITH YOUR DAUGHTER[6]

We need to educate our girls and make them aware of personality traits that are sure to be red flags in a relationship.

Watch out for these traits:

Flattery: Flattery is a manipulation to get a person to behave a particular way. It is different from a compliment. A compliment is meant to make someone else feel good. Flattery's goal is to make the flatterer feel good.

Rudeness: Rudeness to a person in a service position, an elderly person, handicapped individual, or a parent is a bad sign. Those who treat others in a disrespectful way will eventually do the same to a significant other. Choose a person who is kind instead.

Expectantly Giving: This guy spends a lot of money and expects something in return. The individual who believes, "I spent $$$ on you, now you owe me [fill in the blank]," should be kept at arm's length!

Lustful: Lust focuses on self. Love focuses on another.

Arrogant: This guy believes people are lucky to be around or with him and holds the idea that he is "God's gift to women."

Liar/Cheater: Character counts, and no one can change a person like this except for himself. If he hasn't yet, he will end up lying to and cheating on you.

Easily Offended: You will spend all your time apologizing and explaining. It's not worth it.

---

[6]Lori Wildenberg, "12 Dating Warning Signs to Share with Your Daughter," accessed May 24, 2018, https://loriwildenberg.com/2016/03/28/12-dating -warning-signs-to-share-with-your-daughter/.

Always Right: It's his way or the highway. This guy makes ultimatums and blames everyone else for his issues. Just think for a minute what this type of person would be like to live with day in and day out.

Loner: If he has no close friends and very few friends of the same sex, ask yourself why. There may be a reason.

Preener: This guy takes longer than you to get ready. Look out for a guy who is image conscious, all wrapped up in himself, and needs constant validation on his looks, smarts, and on anything in which he participates. The pressure and the emotional drain will be great!

Hypocritical: His words don't match his actions. This man is a big fat fake.

Hurter: If he makes you cry more than laugh, why would anyone want to be in this situation? It would be miserable. Life is too short.

And one bonus thought: If your friends and family don't like him, take heed. These are the people who love you, know you, and care about you.

Girls, if you see these qualities in a guy you may be interested in or who shows an interest in you, run!

Parents, let's train our girls to be discerning and to look beyond the charm. And let's train our sons not to be this dude.

A lying tongue hates those it hurts, and a flattering mouth works ruin. —Proverbs 26:28

CULTURAL CHRISTIANITY INVENTORY

To determine if your child's faith is based on who God is and His Word or if their faith is of our own or our child's making, ask these five questions.

Is an argument for sinful behavior justified in the name of grace while at the expense of truth?

Are feelings the determiner of right and wrong over God's Word?

Is the Bible described as a myth or an outdated irrelevant book?

Do popular books and personalities trump biblical truths?

Does feeling good override conviction?

BRING IT HOME DISCUSSION AND REFLECTION FOR INDIVIDUAL, COUPLE, OR GROUP STUDY

INTRODUCTION: THE DECEPTION ABOUT CONNECTION

Read 1 Corinthians 12:12–31.

Why is it unwise to have the parts work independent of each other?

Relate the body to family life. Why is unity a better quality in families than the characteristic of independence?

What does 1 Corinthians 1:26 mean to you in terms of family life?

How have you (unintentionally) given the message you value independence over family cohesiveness?

How do you feel about asking for help? Describe a time where you needed to rely on others.

How do you feel about giving help? Describe a time when God used you to support someone else.

After reading the introduction what (small) changes can you make today that will increase family connection?

> *Lord, teach me to train my children in a way*
> *that builds family cohesiveness, connection,*
> *and interdependence. Help me to train my kids*
> *to value family relationships over personal*
> *independence. Amen.*

CHAPTER 1: THE ATTACHMENT TRUTH

Read Psalms 18:6; 30:2; 33:20; 46:1, 7–9; 115:9; 121:1; Ecclesiastes 4:9–12; and Hebrews 13:6.

How did you feel about the words *help* and *helper* before reading these passages? How do you feel about them now?

How do you think you have shaped your child's attitude toward giving and receiving help? Look over the different types of connections. Give an example in your life of each type of relationship.

Zero

Toxic

Conditional

Surface

Interdependent

> *Lord, You are my helper. Thank You that I can depend on You. I pray my children learn to go to You in good times and in bad times. Just as You desire to be my helper, I desire to be my child's helper. Amen.*

CHAPTER 2: HEALING THROUGH RELATIONAL TIES

Read Proverbs 23:22; Zephaniah 3:17; and 1 Thessalonians 5:11.

What sort of messages do you consistently send to your children? Are those messages ones that build up and solidify family connections? If not, what will you do differently? If so, share some positive messages you give your children.

What type of self-talk do you model? What type of self-talk do your kids speak?

If their self-talk is negative, how can you help them reframe their thoughts?

Why is identity in Christ important?

Describe the four ways to increase happiness. What will you be more intentional about after learning this?

Look over the 101 Affirmations to Bless Your Child's Heart in the appendix on page 167. Pick seven to speak over your kids this week.

> *Lord, You have put me in a position of great influence over my children. Train me to use this honorable position as a parent for my children's good. Amen.*

CHAPTER 3: MESSAGES THAT BOND

Read James 1:19–20, 26, and 3:1–12.

When speaking to your children are you more likely to:

Empower or enable?

Correct or criticize?

Lecture or listen?

Advise or affirm?

Assume or ask?

Take the Emotional Safety Evaluation in the appendix on page 171. How would you rate the environment in your home?

After reading this chapter what (small) changes can you make today that will increase family connection through the messages you convey?

> *Lord, set a guard over my mouth when my emotions run hot. Give me the self-control to be slow to speak and slow to become angry. I want to show love by demonstrating kindness. Amen.*

CHAPTER 4: CONFLICT DOESN'T MEAN SEPARATION

Read 1 Corinthians 13:11 and 2 Corinthians 10:5.

What do these verses mean to you in terms of conflict?

Why is it important to handle conflict well?

What could you do better?

Look over the six phases on conscience development. How would you characterize your child's conscience development?

Knowing this, how will it impact your interaction with your children?

How does respect cause family members to be more interdependent?

> *Lord, help me to understand my children's frame of reference for making decisions so I am able to parent them well. Stretch and mature my child's faith and mine. Amen.*

CHAPTER 5: DRAWN TOGETHER WITH PEOPLE SMARTS
Read 1 Thessalonians 4:1–12.

How do these verses affect family life and relate to a dependence on God?

Take the Emotional Intelligence Assessment in the appendix on page 172. What did you learn?

Look over Laura Petherbridge's people-pleasing checklist. Are you susceptible to people pleasing? Is your child?

Discuss the five rights. How can this strengthen a child's resolve not to be a people pleaser but a God-pleaser instead?

> *Lord, move me to seek You, Your will, and Your way so my life may be a living sacrifice to You. Amen.*

CHAPTER 6: SIMPLE EVERYDAY CONNECTIONS
Read John 15:1–17.

How can these verses be applied to daily interconnected family life?

Take the Soft Skills Evaluation in the appendix on page 174. What stood out to you?

How would you describe your schedule?

How does Pete's story impact you?

Where can margin be built into your day?

> *Lord, give me a Mary perspective. I want to choose the godly yes rather than just a good yes when it comes to my time. Amen.*

CHAPTER 7: WATCH FOR LOOSE LINKS
Read Luke 10:38–41.

How can distractions loosen family and faith ties?

After reading this chapter, how can you cement sibling relationships among your children?

Why is empathy better than sympathy?

What are the six ways to help your child navigate difficult or even devastating life experiences?

Lord, help me to be present and to be aware of the moments or events that can draw my family apart and away from You. Amen.

CHAPTER 8: THE ALL-ABOUT-ME DISCONNECT

Read Philippians 2:1–4.

What message can parents take from these verses in Philippians?

How is independence linked to entitlement?

How does self-sufficiency get in the way of God dependence and interdependent relationships?

What is the difference between responsible and independent?

Lord, draw my kids close to You. Take away their bent for independence and replace it with a God-dependence and a desire for interdependence among Your people. Amen.

CHAPTER 9: THE SYNERGY OF EFFECTIVE LEADERSHIP

Read 1 Corinthians 3:4–5.

What was Paul attempting to communicate in these verses? What can your children learn from these words?

Look over the tips for raising kids who are passionately purpose driven. What do you do well? What can you do differently?

What do you value, peacemaking or peacekeeping? What do you encourage? Is it the same or different? If different, why?

Who do your kids look up to? Why?

Lord, give my kids discerning eyes to see those who are good and godly leaders. I pray they follow those who follow You. Give my children wisdom to make decisions that honor You. Amen.

CHAPTER 10: MAKE NECESSARY ADJUSTMENTS

Read Daniel 2:21–22.

How do these verses relate to family life?

If you are a single or stepparent or are separated by generations or distance, interdependence is still possible. What can you do to tighten your bond with your child or grandchild?

> *Lord, life is always changing. Help me to adjust to the changes You have allowed to enter my life. Amen.*

CHAPTER 11: SUPERNATURAL CONNECTION

Read Deuteronomy 6:1–9.

Take the Cultural Christianity Inventory in the appendix on page 181. What did you discover?

How do you communicate your faith to your children?

What are some of your God stories? Have you shared them with your family?

Review Tim Shoemaker's crash course on why bad things happen with your kids.

When has fear trumped faith in your journey? When has faith been the victor?

> *Lord, let me be the example of how to trust you in the fearful moments. Remind me of the times You showed Yourself so I may tell the stories to my children. Amen.*

CONCLUSION: THE DECLARATION OF INTERDEPENDENCE

Look over the Declaration of Interdependence on page 164, and discuss it with your family.

Create a plaque with these principles on it.

Add some of your own. Title it The [your name here] Family Declaration of Interdependence.

Father, thank You for Your love. Thank You that Jesus reminds us of the two most important commands, to love You and to love others.Amen.

One of the teachers of the law came and heard them debating. Noticing that Jesus had given them a good answer, he asked him, "Of all the commandments, which is the most important?" "The most important one," answered Jesus, "is this: 'Hear, O Israel: The Lord our God, the Lord is one. Love the Lord your God with all your heart and with all your soul and with all your mind and with all your strength.' The second is this: 'Love your neighbor as yourself.' There is no commandment greater than these."
—Mark 12:28–31

INDEX

SUGGESTED RESOURCES FOR PARENTS, GRANDPARENTS, AND PASTORS

Online Resources

    1Corinthians13Parenting.com

    LoriWildenberg.com

    AFathersWalk.org

    CelebrateKids.com

    Expeditionba.com

    Facebook.com/MomsTogether

    FamilyFestMinistries.org

    FamTime.com

    HealingForTheSoul.org

    LauraPetherbridge.com

    Mops.org

    TheSingleMomkc.org

Print Resources

Forsaken God? Remembering the Goodness of God Our Culture Has Forgotten by Janet Thompson

Parenting Unchained: Overcoming the Ten Deceptions That Shackle Christian Parents by Jim Dempsey

Screens and Teens: Connecting with Our Kids in a Wireless World by Kathy Koch

Raising Big Kids with Supernatural Love by Lori Wildenberg and Becky Danielson

Raising Little Kids with Big Love by Lori Wildenberg and Becky Danielson

Messy Journey: How Grace and Truth Offer the Prodigal a Way Home by Lori Wildenberg

The Smart Stepmom: Practical Steps to Help You Thrive by Ron L. Deal and Laura Petherbridge

About the Author

Lori Wildenberg, mom of four, is passionate about helping families build connections that last a lifetime. As a licensed parent-family educator, she is professionally equipped to encourage and empower moms and dads to be the parents their children need.

With more than twenty-five years' experience working with parents and kids in both faith-based and secular settings, her philosophy is focused on developing a child's heart and character while creating a family system that is interdependent and dependent on God.

Lori has written five parenting books, with *The Messy Life of Parenting: Powerful and Practical Ways to Strengthen Family Connections* being her most recent. She is the author of *Messy Journey: How Grace and Truth Offer the Prodigal a Way Home* and coauthor of *Raising Big Kids with Supernatural Love*, *Raising Little Kids with Big Love*, and *Empowered Parents: Putting Faith First*.

A national speaker, Lori is a member of the Advanced Writers and Speakers Association. She is cofounder of the 1 Corinthians 13 Parenting Ministry, a resource site for parents and those who work with families. She is on staff as a parent coach at Healing for the Soul, volunteers her time mentoring women, and is the lead mentor mom at the Moms Together Facebook community page and group. She is also a freelance writer for a number of online Christian parenting magazines.

Lori is an avid hiker who describes her perfect day as starting with a hike with her husband, their four kids, and one daughter-in-love. It concludes with a movie, popcorn, and milk duds to be shared with Tom, her husband of thirty-five years. The Wildenberg home is nestled in the foothills of the Rocky Mountains. For more information, visit loriwildenberg.com.